Twice Exceptional: Navigating Life with Autism and Gomez Lopez Hernandez Syndrome

Travis Breeding

Published by Travis Breeding, 2024.

While every precaution has been taken in the preparation of this book, the publisher assumes no responsibility for errors or omissions, or for damages resulting from the use of the information contained herein.

TWICE EXCEPTIONAL: NAVIGATING LIFE WITH AUTISM AND GOMEZ LOPEZ HERNANDEZ SYNDROME

First edition. February 21, 2024.

Copyright © 2024 Travis Breeding.

ISBN: 979-8224021543

Written by Travis Breeding.

Also by Travis Breeding

Harmony in Flux: Navigating Bi-Polar Brilliance
The Friendship Rainbow
The Great Kindergarten Adventure: A Story about Going to School with Autism
The Magic Forest Adventure
Unlocking Brilliance: Navigating Autism and Applied Behavior Analysis Towards a Radiant Future
Decoding Love: Navigating Dating and Relationships on the Autism Spectrum
Echoes of a Late Diagnosis: Unveiling the Spectrum Within
From Theory to Practice: Implementing Effective Autism Interventions St
The Amazing Adventures of Aiden and His Asperger's Superpowers
The Magical Adventures of Lily and the Enchanted Forest
Unlocking Potential: A Journey Of Discovery Through ABA Therapy
Unlocking Potential: Navigating Employment for Neurodiverse Talent
Unlocking the Spectrum: A Journey through Applied Behavior Analysis from an Autistic Perspective
Unlocking The Spectrum: Navigating The Complexity Of Autism With Advanced Strategies And Insights
Beyond The Spectrum: Insights From Autistic Adults
Beyond The Stereotypes
Breaking Barriers: Navigating Autism With Therapeutic Insight
Celebrating Neurodiversity

Watch for more at breedingautismconsulting.com.

Table of Contents

Chapter 1: Embracing Neurodiversity In The Autism Community

Neurodiversity is a concept that has gained increasing recognition and importance in recent years. It refers to the idea that neurological differences, such as autism, ADHD, and dyslexia, are simply natural variations of the human brain rather than disorders or deficits. This perspective challenges the traditional medical model of viewing neurodivergent individuals as needing to be fixed or cured, and instead promotes acceptance, understanding, and celebration of these differences. In this article, we will explore the concept of neurodiversity and its significance in society. We will discuss the autism spectrum, the importance of celebrating differences, the role of advocacy, embracing neurodiversity in the workplace and education, addressing disparities and challenges faced by marginalized neurodivergent individuals, recognizing unique strengths, challenging misconceptions, and ultimately building a more empathetic and inclusive society for all.

Understanding Neurodiversity: What Does it Mean?

Neurodiversity is a term that was coined by Australian sociologist Judy Singer in the late 1990s. It is based on the idea that neurological differences are simply natural variations of the human brain and should be accepted and celebrated rather than pathologized. Neurodivergent individuals are those who have neurological differences such as autism, ADHD, dyslexia, and other conditions. On the other hand, neurotypical individuals are those whose neurological development falls within the typical range.

The concept of neurodiversity challenges the traditional medical model of viewing neurodivergent individuals as having disorders or deficits that need to be fixed or cured. Instead, it recognizes that these differences are a part of human diversity and should be respected and accommodated. It promotes the idea that neurodivergent individuals have unique strengths and perspectives that can contribute to society in valuable ways.

The Autism Spectrum: A Spectrum of Differences

Autism is one of the most well-known and widely discussed neurodivergent conditions. It is a developmental disorder that affects communication, social interaction, and behavior. Autism is often referred to as a spectrum disorder because it can manifest in a wide range of ways and with varying degrees of severity.

Some individuals with autism may have difficulty with social interactions and communication, while others may have exceptional abilities in certain areas such as mathematics or music. Some individuals may have sensory sensitivities or repetitive behaviors, while others may not. The autism spectrum is diverse and encompasses a wide range of experiences and abilities.

It is important to recognize that each individual with autism is unique and has their own strengths, challenges, and needs. By understanding and accepting this diversity, we can create a more inclusive society that values and supports all individuals, regardless of their neurodivergent status.

Celebrating Differences: Why Neurodiversity Matters

Celebrating differences is crucial for creating a more inclusive society. When we embrace neurodiversity, we recognize that every individual has unique strengths, perspectives, and contributions to make. By valuing these differences, we can create a society that is more innovative, creative, and compassionate.

Neurodivergent individuals often have unique talents and abilities that can be harnessed for the benefit of society. For example, individuals with autism may have exceptional attention to detail, pattern recognition skills, or the ability to think outside the box. By providing opportunities for these individuals to showcase their strengths, we can tap into their potential and create a more diverse and dynamic workforce.

Furthermore, celebrating neurodiversity helps to challenge societal norms and stereotypes. It promotes the idea that there is no one "normal" way of being and encourages acceptance of all individuals, regardless of their neurological differences. This can lead to greater empathy, understanding, and inclusion for all members of society.

The Importance of Acceptance: Building a More Inclusive Society

Stigma and discrimination against neurodivergent individuals can have significant negative effects on their well-being and quality of life. Many neurodivergent individuals face challenges in areas such as education, employment, and social relationships due to the lack of acceptance and understanding in society.

Stigma and discrimination can lead to feelings of isolation, low self-esteem, and mental health issues. It can also limit opportunities for neurodivergent individuals to fully participate in society and reach their potential. By promoting acceptance and inclusion, we can create a society that values and supports all individuals, regardless of their neurological differences.

Acceptance means recognizing that neurodivergent individuals have unique strengths, challenges, and needs. It means providing accommodations and support to ensure that all individuals can fully participate in all aspects of life. It also means challenging stereotypes and promoting accurate information about neurodiversity.

The Role of Advocacy: Supporting Neurodivergent Individuals

Advocacy plays a crucial role in supporting neurodivergent individuals and promoting acceptance and inclusion in society. Advocacy involves speaking up for the rights and needs of neurodivergent individuals, raising awareness about neurodiversity, and working towards systemic change.

There are many advocacy organizations and resources available to support neurodivergent individuals and their families. These organizations provide information, support, and resources to help navigate the challenges faced by neurodivergent individuals in areas such as education, employment, healthcare, and social services.

Advocacy also involves promoting policies and practices that support neurodiversity. This includes advocating for inclusive education environments, workplace accommodations, accessible healthcare services, and community support networks. By working together to advocate for change, we can create a more inclusive society that values and supports all individuals.

Embracing Neurodiversity in the Workplace: Accommodations and Opportunities

Embracing neurodiversity in the workplace is not only the right thing to do, but it also makes good business sense. Neurodivergent individuals often have unique talents and abilities that can contribute to the success of organizations. By providing accommodations and opportunities for neurodivergent individuals, employers can tap into this potential and create a more diverse and innovative workforce.

Accommodations in the workplace can include things like flexible work schedules, sensory-friendly environments, clear communication strategies, and task modifications. These accommodations can help neurodivergent individuals to thrive in their roles and reach their full potential.

In addition to accommodations, it is important to provide opportunities for neurodivergent individuals to showcase their strengths and talents. This can include creating mentorship programs, providing training and development opportunities, and fostering a culture of inclusion and acceptance.

Education and Neurodiversity: Creating Inclusive Learning Environments

Creating inclusive learning environments is essential for supporting neurodivergent students and promoting their success. Inclusive education means providing all students, regardless of their neurodivergent status, with the support and accommodations they need to fully participate in the classroom.

Inclusive classrooms recognize that each student is unique and has their own strengths, challenges, and needs. They provide a variety of teaching strategies, materials, and assessments to meet the diverse learning needs of all students.

Some strategies for creating inclusive classrooms include providing visual supports, breaking tasks into smaller steps, allowing for flexible seating arrangements, providing extra time for assignments or tests, and fostering a culture of acceptance and understanding.

By creating inclusive learning environments, we can ensure that all students have equal access to education and the opportunity to reach their full potential.

The Intersection of Race, Gender, and Neurodiversity: Addressing Disparities and Challenges

Neurodivergent individuals who are also marginalized in other ways, such as by race or gender, face unique challenges and disparities. Intersectionality refers to the ways in which different aspects of a person's identity can intersect and interact to create unique experiences and challenges.

For example, neurodivergent individuals who are also people of color may face additional barriers and discrimination due to racism and ableism. Similarly, neurodivergent individuals who are also women may face gender-based discrimination and stereotypes that compound the challenges they face.

It is important to recognize and address these disparities and challenges in advocacy and support efforts. This includes promoting intersectionality in advocacy organizations, policies, and practices. By taking an intersectional approach, we can ensure that the needs and experiences of all neurodivergent individuals are recognized and addressed.

Celebrating Strengths: Recognizing the Unique Talents of Neurodivergent Individuals

Neurodivergent individuals often have unique strengths and talents that should be recognized and celebrated. For example, individuals with autism may have exceptional attention to detail, pattern recognition skills, or the ability to think outside the box. Individuals with ADHD may have high levels of creativity, energy, and problem-solving abilities.

By recognizing and celebrating these strengths, we can create a society that values and supports all individuals, regardless of their neurological differences. This can lead to greater opportunities for neurodivergent individuals to showcase their talents and contribute to society in meaningful ways.

It is important to move away from a deficit-based perspective that focuses solely on the challenges faced by neurodivergent individuals. Instead, we should focus on their strengths and abilities and provide opportunities for them to thrive.

Overcoming Stigma: Challenging Misconceptions About Autism and Neurodiversity

There are many misconceptions and stereotypes about autism and neurodiversity that contribute to stigma and discrimination. These misconceptions can lead to misunderstandings, fear, and exclusion of neurodivergent individuals.

One common misconception is that all individuals with autism are nonverbal or have intellectual disabilities. In reality, autism is a spectrum disorder and individuals with autism have a wide range of abilities and strengths.

Another misconception is that neurodivergent individuals are not capable of forming meaningful relationships or contributing to society. This is simply not true. Neurodivergent individuals have unique perspectives and talents that can enrich our communities and contribute to the success of organizations.

Challenging these misconceptions and promoting accurate information about autism and neurodiversity is crucial for creating a more inclusive society. This can be done through education, awareness campaigns, and promoting positive portrayals of neurodivergent individuals in the media.

Moving Forward: Building a More Empathetic and Inclusive Society for All

In conclusion, neurodiversity is an important concept that challenges traditional views of neurological differences as disorders or deficits. By embracing neurodiversity, we can create a more inclusive society that values and supports all individuals, regardless of their neurological differences.

This requires promoting acceptance, understanding, and celebration of neurodivergent individuals. It also involves providing accommodations and opportunities in areas such as education and employment, addressing disparities faced by marginalized neurodivergent individuals, recognizing and celebrating their unique strengths, challenging misconceptions, and promoting accurate information.

Building a more empathetic and inclusive society requires the collective effort of individuals, communities, organizations, and policymakers. By working together, we can create a society that values diversity in all its forms and ensures that every individual has the opportunity to thrive.

Chapter 2: Gomez Lopez Hernandez Syndrome

Gomez Lopez Hernandez Syndrome (GLHS) is a rare genetic disorder that affects individuals from birth. It is characterized by a range of physical and developmental symptoms, including intellectual disability, facial abnormalities, and delayed growth. Understanding GLHS is crucial for healthcare professionals, researchers, and families, as it can help improve diagnosis, treatment, and support for individuals with this syndrome.

What is Gomez Lopez Hernandez Syndrome?

Gomez Lopez Hernandez Syndrome is a genetic disorder that was first described in 1974 by Dr. Juan Gomez Lopez and Dr. Victor Hernandez Garcia. It is also known as cerebellar hypoplasia with endosteal sclerosis (CHES) or cerebellar hypoplasia with cutis congenita (CHCC). GLHS is characterized by a range of physical and developmental symptoms, including intellectual disability, facial abnormalities, and delayed growth.

The Causes and Symptoms of Gomez Lopez Hernandez Syndrome

The exact cause of Gomez Lopez Hernandez Syndrome is not yet fully understood. However, it is believed to be caused by mutations in the KIF7 gene, which plays a role in the development of the cerebellum and other parts of the body. These mutations disrupt the normal development of the brain and other organs, leading to the symptoms associated with GLHS.

The symptoms of Gomez Lopez Hernandez Syndrome can vary widely from person to person. Some common physical symptoms include facial abnormalities such as a small head size, low-set ears, and a cleft palate. Individuals with GLHS may also have skeletal abnormalities, such as short stature and abnormal bone development.

The Prevalence of Gomez Lopez Hernandez Syndrome

Gomez Lopez Hernandez Syndrome is an extremely rare disorder, with only a few dozen cases reported worldwide. Due to its rarity, it is difficult to determine the exact prevalence of GLHS. However, it is believed to affect both males and females equally.

Diagnosis and Treatment Options for Gomez Lopez Hernandez Syndrome

Diagnosing Gomez Lopez Hernandez Syndrome can be challenging, as the symptoms can vary widely from person to person. However, there are some diagnostic criteria that can help healthcare professionals identify individuals with GLHS. These criteria include physical examination, genetic testing, and imaging studies.

Currently, there is no cure for Gomez Lopez Hernandez Syndrome. However, there are treatment options available to manage the symptoms and improve the quality of life for individuals with GLHS. These treatment options may include physical therapy, speech therapy, and educational interventions.

How Gomez Lopez Hernandez Syndrome Affects Cognitive Development

Gomez Lopez Hernandez Syndrome can have a significant impact on cognitive development. Many individuals with GLHS have intellectual disability, ranging from mild to severe. They may have difficulties with learning, problem-solving, and communication.

In addition to intellectual disability, individuals with Gomez Lopez Hernandez Syndrome may also experience challenges in academic and social settings. They may have difficulty with attention and concentration, making it harder for them to learn and participate in classroom activities. They may also struggle with social interactions and may have difficulty forming and maintaining relationships.

The Relationship Between Gomez Lopez Hernandez Syndrome and Autism

There is some overlap between Gomez Lopez Hernandez Syndrome and autism spectrum disorder (ASD). Some individuals with GLHS may also exhibit symptoms of ASD, such as social communication difficulties and repetitive behaviors. However, it is important to note that not all individuals with GLHS will have a diagnosis of ASD.

While there are similarities between GLHS and autism, there are also some key differences. For example, individuals with GLHS typically have physical abnormalities, such as facial abnormalities and skeletal abnormalities, which are not typically seen in individuals with autism. Additionally, the underlying genetic causes of GLHS and autism are different.

How to Manage Behavioral Challenges Associated with Gomez Lopez Hernandez Syndrome

Individuals with Gomez Lopez Hernandez Syndrome may experience a range of behavioral challenges. These challenges can include aggression, self-injurious behaviors, and difficulties with impulse control. Managing these behaviors can be challenging for families and caregivers.

There are several strategies that can be helpful in managing behavioral challenges associated with GLHS. These may include creating a structured and predictable environment, using visual supports to help with communication and understanding, and implementing positive behavior support strategies. It is important to work closely with healthcare professionals and behavior specialists to develop an individualized behavior management plan.

The Importance of Early Intervention for Gomez Lopez Hernandez Syndrome

Early intervention is crucial for individuals with Gomez Lopez Hernandez Syndrome. Research has shown that early intervention can lead to improved outcomes in terms of cognitive development, communication skills, and social interactions.

Early intervention for GLHS may include therapies such as physical therapy, occupational therapy, speech therapy, and educational interventions. These interventions can help individuals with GLHS develop the skills they need to reach their full potential.

Coping Strategies for Families of Individuals with Gomez Lopez Hernandez Syndrome

Families of individuals with Gomez Lopez Hernandez Syndrome may face unique challenges. It can be difficult to navigate the healthcare system, find appropriate resources and support, and manage the day-to-day care of a child with GLHS.

One important coping strategy for families is to seek out support from other families who are going through similar experiences. Support groups and online communities can provide a valuable source of information, advice, and emotional support. It is also important for families to take care of themselves and seek out respite care when needed.

Resources and Support for Those Affected by Gomez Lopez Hernandez Syndrome

There are several organizations and support groups that provide resources and support for individuals with Gomez Lopez Hernandez Syndrome and their families. These organizations can provide information about the latest research, connect families with healthcare professionals who specialize in GLHS, and offer support through online communities and local support groups.

In addition to these organizations, there are also resources available for education and advocacy. These resources can help families navigate the educational system, access appropriate services and supports, and advocate for their child's needs.

The Future of Research and Treatment for Gomez Lopez Hernandez Syndrome

Research on Gomez Lopez Hernandez Syndrome is ongoing, with scientists working to better understand the underlying causes of the disorder and develop new treatment options. Some current areas of research include studying the role of the KIF7 gene in brain development, exploring potential therapies to improve cognitive function, and investigating the overlap between GLHS and other neurodevelopmental disorders.

While there is currently no cure for Gomez Lopez Hernandez Syndrome, advances in research and treatment offer hope for the future. Continued support for research and advocacy is crucial to improve outcomes for individuals with GLHS and their families.

Gomez Lopez Hernandez Syndrome is a rare genetic disorder that affects individuals from birth. Understanding GLHS is important for healthcare professionals, researchers, and families, as it can help improve diagnosis, treatment, and support for individuals with this syndrome. While there is currently no cure for GLHS, there are treatment options available to manage the symptoms and improve quality of life. Continued research and support are crucial to improve outcomes for individuals with GLHS and their families.

Chapter 3: The Importance of Sharing Your Story: Why Everyone Should Write an Autobiography

Personal narratives are stories that individuals share about their own lives, experiences, and perspectives. These stories can take various forms, such as autobiographies, memoirs, or personal essays. They provide a unique insight into the author's thoughts, emotions, and personal growth. Sharing personal stories is important because it allows individuals to connect with others, find their voice, reflect on their experiences, leave a legacy, and break free from negative self-perceptions. Autobiographical writing has numerous benefits, including therapeutic effects, building empathy and understanding, empowering oneself, finding inspiration, honoring one's experiences, and building resilience.

Discovering Your Unique Voice: How Writing Your Story Can Help You Find Your Identity

Finding your voice is crucial for personal growth and self-discovery. Writing your story can be a powerful tool in this process. When you write about your experiences and emotions, you are forced to confront your own thoughts and beliefs. This process allows you to explore your identity and values more deeply. By putting your thoughts into words, you gain a better understanding of who you are and what matters to you.

Writing your story also helps you discover your unique voice by allowing you to express yourself authentically. When you write from a place of honesty and vulnerability, your true voice emerges. This is the voice that resonates with others and makes your story compelling. To find your unique voice, it is important to write without fear of judgment or comparison. Embrace your individuality and let your story unfold naturally.

Reflection and Healing: The Therapeutic Benefits of Autobiographical Writing

Writing can be a therapeutic process that promotes healing and self-discovery. When you reflect on your life experiences through autobiographical writing, you gain a deeper understanding of yourself and the events that have shaped you. This reflection allows you to make sense of past traumas or challenges and find meaning in your journey.

Autobiographical writing provides a safe space to explore and process emotions. By putting your thoughts and feelings on paper, you can release pent-up emotions and gain a sense of relief. This process can be particularly helpful for individuals who have experienced trauma or difficult life events. Writing allows them to confront their pain, acknowledge their emotions, and begin the healing process.

There are numerous examples of how autobiographical writing has promoted healing. For instance, many individuals who have experienced loss or grief have found solace in writing about their experiences. By sharing their stories, they not only find support from others who have gone through similar experiences but also gain a sense of closure and acceptance.

Leaving a Legacy: Why Your Story Matters to Future Generations

Leaving a legacy is an important aspect of human existence. We all want to be remembered and have our lives make a lasting impact. Autobiographical writing provides a way to leave behind a piece of ourselves for future generations to learn from and connect with.

When you write your story, you are preserving your unique perspective and experiences for future generations. Your story becomes a part of history, offering insights into a particular time, place, or culture. It allows future generations to understand the challenges, triumphs, and lessons learned by those who came before them.

Famous autobiographies such as "The Diary of Anne Frank" and "The Autobiography of Malcolm X" have left a lasting impact on society. These books have provided valuable insights into the lives of individuals who faced adversity and fought for justice. Their stories continue to inspire and educate readers today.

Connecting with Others: The Role of Autobiography in Building Empathy and Understanding

Sharing personal stories is a powerful way to build empathy and understanding between individuals. When we hear someone's personal narrative, we gain insight into their experiences, emotions, and perspectives. This understanding allows us to connect with them on a deeper level and fosters empathy.

Listening to others' stories helps us recognize our shared humanity. It reminds us that we all have struggles, dreams, and desires. By hearing diverse stories, we become more open-minded and accepting of different perspectives. This empathy and understanding can lead to positive social change and a more inclusive society.

Autobiographical writing has played a significant role in building connections between people. For example, the memoir "Educated" by Tara Westover has sparked conversations about the importance of education and the power of resilience. By sharing her story, Westover has inspired readers to reflect on their own lives and consider the impact of education on personal growth.

Overcoming Shame and Stigma: How Sharing Your Story Can Help You Break Free from

Negative Self-Perceptions

Shame and stigma can have a profound impact on an individual's self-perception and mental well-being. However, sharing your story can be a powerful way to break free from these negative self-perceptions. When you share your experiences, you realize that you are not alone in your struggles. This realization can help alleviate feelings of shame and isolation.

Autobiographical writing allows individuals to reclaim their narratives and challenge societal norms or expectations. By sharing their stories, they can challenge stigmatizing beliefs or misconceptions and promote understanding and acceptance.

There are numerous examples of how autobiographical writing has helped people overcome shame and stigma. For instance, the memoir "Hunger" by Roxane Gay explores the author's experiences with body image, trauma, and societal expectations. By sharing her story, Gay challenges societal norms around body size and promotes body positivity.

Empowering Yourself: The Transformative Effects of Owning Your Story

Owning your story is a powerful act of self-empowerment. When you embrace your experiences, both positive and negative, you take control of your narrative. This ownership allows you to define yourself on your own terms and reject societal expectations or judgments.

Autobiographical writing provides a platform for individuals to share their stories and take ownership of their experiences. By writing about their triumphs, challenges, and personal growth, they empower themselves and inspire others to do the same.

There are numerous examples of how autobiographical writing has helped people feel empowered. For instance, the memoir "Wild" by Cheryl Strayed chronicles the author's journey of self-discovery and healing through hiking the Pacific Crest Trail. By sharing her story, Strayed empowers readers to embrace their own journeys and find strength in adversity.

Finding Inspiration: How Reading Other People's Autobiographies Can Help You Grow and Learn

Reading autobiographies can be a source of inspiration and personal growth. When we read about other people's experiences, we gain new perspectives and insights that can help us navigate our own lives.

Autobiographies provide a window into the lives of individuals who have faced challenges, overcome adversity, or achieved great success. By reading about their journeys, we can learn valuable lessons and apply them to our own lives.

There are numerous examples of autobiographies that have inspired readers. For instance, "The Diary of a Young Girl" by Anne Frank has inspired millions with its message of hope and resilience in the face of unimaginable adversity. By reading Anne Frank's story, readers gain a new appreciation for the power of optimism and the strength of the human spirit.

Honoring Your Experiences: Recognizing the Value of Your Life Journey

Every individual's life journey is unique and valuable. Autobiographical writing provides a way to honor and recognize the value of your experiences. By reflecting on your journey and sharing your story, you acknowledge the lessons learned, the growth achieved, and the impact you have had on others.

Autobiographical writing allows you to celebrate your accomplishments and milestones. It provides an opportunity to express gratitude for the people, places, and experiences that have shaped you.

By recognizing the value of your life journey, you gain a sense of purpose and fulfillment.

There are numerous examples of how autobiographical writing has helped people recognize the value of their experiences. For instance, the memoir "Eat, Pray, Love" by Elizabeth Gilbert chronicles the author's journey of self-discovery and spiritual awakening. By sharing her story, Gilbert encourages readers to embrace their own journeys and find meaning in their experiences.

Building Resilience: The Role of Autobiography in Coping with Life Challenges and Adversity

Resilience is the ability to bounce back from challenges and adversity. Autobiographical writing can play a significant role in building resilience by allowing individuals to reflect on their past experiences and find strength in their ability to overcome obstacles.

When you write about your challenges and how you have overcome them, you gain a sense of perspective and resilience. This reflection allows you to recognize your own strength and resilience, which can be empowering during difficult times.

There are numerous examples of how autobiographical writing has helped people cope with life challenges and adversity. For instance, the memoir "The Glass Castle" by Jeannette Walls chronicles the author's upbringing in a dysfunctional family and her journey to overcome poverty and achieve success. By sharing her story, Walls inspires readers to persevere in the face of adversity and find strength within themselves.

Encouraging Everyone to Embrace the Power of Narrative and Share Their Story with the World

In conclusion, autobiographical writing has numerous benefits that can positively impact individuals and society as a whole. It allows individuals to discover their unique voice, reflect on their experiences, heal from past traumas, leave a lasting legacy, build empathy and understanding, overcome shame and stigma, empower themselves, find inspiration, honor their experiences, and build resilience.

It is important for everyone to embrace the power of narrative and share their stories with the world. By sharing our personal narratives, we can connect with others, inspire change, and leave a lasting impact. Our stories matter, and they have the power to shape the world in meaningful ways. So, let us all embrace the power of autobiographical writing and share our stories with the world.

Chapter 4: The Power of Perseverance: My Journey to Achieving My Dreams

Perseverance is the ability to persist in the face of challenges, setbacks, and obstacles. It is the determination to keep going, even when things get tough. Perseverance is a crucial trait to have when it comes to achieving your dreams because it allows you to overcome the inevitable hurdles that will come your way.

Without perseverance, it is easy to give up when faced with difficulties. However, those who persevere are able to push through and continue working towards their goals. Perseverance is what separates those who achieve their dreams from those who fall short.

When you persevere, you develop resilience and determination. You learn to adapt and find solutions to problems. Perseverance also helps you build character and develop a strong work ethic. It teaches you the value of hard work and dedication.

Overcoming Obstacles: My Journey to Success

I have personally experienced the power of perseverance in my own journey towards success. Like many others, I faced numerous obstacles and challenges along the way. However, I refused to let these setbacks define me or deter me from my goals.

One of the biggest obstacles I faced was financial hardship. I came from a low-income background and had limited resources to pursue my dreams. However, I was determined to overcome this obstacle and find a way to make my dreams a reality.

I worked multiple jobs while attending school full-time, saving every penny I could towards my goals. It was not easy, and there were many times when I felt overwhelmed and discouraged. However, I reminded myself of why I started and kept pushing forward.

Through perseverance, I was able to secure scholarships and grants that helped alleviate some of the financial burden. I also sought out mentors and advisors who provided guidance and support along the way. With their help and my unwavering determination, I was able to overcome the obstacles in my path and achieve my dreams.

Defining Your Dreams: How to Set Goals and Stay Focused

In order to persevere, it is important to have a clear vision of what you want to achieve. This starts with defining your dreams and setting goals. By having a clear direction, you can stay focused and motivated even when faced with challenges.

To define your dreams, take some time to reflect on what truly makes you happy and fulfilled. What are your passions and interests? What are your strengths and talents? Once you have a clear understanding of what you want to achieve, set specific, measurable, achievable, relevant, and time-bound (SMART) goals.

It is also important to break down your goals into smaller, manageable tasks. This allows you to track your progress and celebrate small victories along the way. Additionally, it helps prevent overwhelm and keeps you motivated.

To stay focused on your goals, it can be helpful to create a vision board or write down your goals and keep them somewhere visible. Surround yourself with reminders of what you are working towards. This will serve as a constant source of motivation and help you stay on track.

The Role of Resilience in Perseverance: How to Bounce Back from Failure

Resilience is the ability to bounce back from failure or setbacks. It is an essential trait to have when it comes to perseverance because it allows you to learn from your mistakes and keep moving forward.

Failure is inevitable on the path to success. It is important to remember that failure does not define you or your abilities. Instead, it is an opportunity for growth and learning. By embracing failure as a stepping stone towards success, you can develop resilience and continue working towards your goals.

One strategy for bouncing back from failure is reframing your mindset. Instead of viewing failure as a negative outcome, see it as a valuable learning experience. Ask yourself what you can learn from the situation and how you can improve moving forward.

It is also important to practice self-compassion and be kind to yourself when faced with failure. Treat yourself with the same kindness and understanding you would offer a friend. Remember that everyone makes mistakes and experiences setbacks. It is how you respond to these challenges that matters.

The Power of Positive Thinking: How to Stay Motivated and Optimistic

Positive thinking plays a crucial role in perseverance. When you have a positive mindset, you are more likely to stay motivated and optimistic, even when faced with challenges.

Positive thinking involves focusing on the good in every situation and believing in your ability to overcome obstacles. It is about reframing negative thoughts and replacing them with positive ones. By doing so, you can shift your perspective and maintain a sense of hope and optimism.

One way to cultivate positive thinking is through daily affirmations. These are positive statements that you repeat to yourself regularly. For example, you might say, "I am capable of achieving my goals" or "I am resilient and can overcome any challenge." By repeating these affirmations, you can reprogram your mind to think positively.

Another strategy for staying motivated and optimistic is surrounding yourself with positive influences. This includes spending time with supportive friends and family members who believe in your abilities. It also involves consuming positive content, such as books, podcasts, or videos that inspire and uplift you.

The Importance of Hard Work: How to Stay Committed to Your Goals

Perseverance requires hard work and dedication. It is not enough to simply have dreams and goals; you must be willing to put in the effort required to achieve them.

Hard work involves consistently showing up and putting in the necessary time and energy towards your goals. It means being disciplined and committed, even when it feels challenging or overwhelming.

To stay committed to your goals, it can be helpful to create a schedule or routine that allows you to prioritize your tasks. Set aside dedicated time each day or week to work towards your goals. Treat this time as non-negotiable and hold yourself accountable.

It is also important to stay motivated and inspired. Find ways to keep your passion alive and remind yourself of why you started in the first place. This might involve seeking out mentors or role models who have achieved similar goals, reading books or articles related to your field, or attending conferences or workshops.

Cultivating a Support System: How to Surround

Yourself with Positive Influences

Having a support system is crucial when it comes to perseverance. Surrounding yourself with positive influences can provide encouragement, guidance, and motivation during challenging times.

A support system can include friends, family members, mentors, or colleagues who believe in your abilities and support your goals. These individuals can offer valuable advice, provide a listening ear, or simply be there to cheer you on.

To cultivate a support system, it is important to be proactive in seeking out positive relationships and influences. Attend networking events or join professional organizations related to your field. Reach out to individuals who inspire you and ask if they would be willing to mentor or guide you.

It is also important to be a supportive friend and offer encouragement to others. By being there for others, you are more likely to receive support in return. Building strong relationships based on trust and mutual support is key to maintaining perseverance.

The Role of Self-Care in Perseverance: How to Maintain Your Physical and Mental Health

Self-care is often overlooked when it comes to perseverance, but it plays a crucial role in maintaining physical and mental health. Taking care of yourself allows you to recharge and stay resilient in the face of challenges.

Physical self-care involves prioritizing activities that promote physical well-being, such as exercise, healthy eating, and getting enough sleep. It also includes taking breaks and allowing yourself time to rest and relax.

Mental self-care involves engaging in activities that promote mental well-being, such as practicing mindfulness or meditation, journaling, or engaging in hobbies or activities that bring you joy. It also involves setting boundaries and saying no to things that drain your energy or cause unnecessary stress.

By prioritizing self-care, you are better equipped to handle the challenges that come your way. You have more energy, focus, and resilience. Taking care of yourself is not selfish; it is necessary for long-term success and fulfillment.

The Benefits of Perseverance: How to Achieve Success and Fulfillment

Perseverance offers numerous benefits when it comes to achieving success and fulfillment. By persevering through challenges, you develop resilience, determination, and a strong work ethic. These traits not only help you achieve your goals but also contribute to personal growth and development.

Perseverance also allows you to overcome obstacles and setbacks that may arise along the way. Instead of giving up when faced with difficulties, you find solutions and keep moving forward. This ability to adapt and problem-solve is crucial in today's ever-changing world.

Additionally, perseverance leads to a sense of accomplishment and fulfillment. When you achieve your goals after persevering through challenges, you experience a deep sense of satisfaction and pride. This fuels your motivation to continue setting new goals and working towards them.

Lessons Learned: Reflections on My Journey to Achieving My Dreams

Looking back on my own journey towards achieving my dreams, I have learned several valuable lessons. First and foremost, I have learned the importance of perseverance. Without it, I would not have been able to overcome the obstacles in my path and achieve my goals.

I have also learned the power of resilience and positive thinking. By bouncing back from failure and maintaining a positive mindset, I was able to stay motivated and optimistic even during challenging times.

Furthermore, I have learned the importance of self-care and having a support system. Taking care of myself physically and mentally allowed me to stay resilient and maintain my focus. Having a support system provided me with encouragement, guidance, and motivation when I needed it most.

The Power of Perseverance and How to Apply it to Your Life

Perseverance is a powerful trait that can help you achieve your dreams and find success and fulfillment. By overcoming obstacles, defining your dreams, staying focused, bouncing back from failure, maintaining a positive mindset, working hard, cultivating a support system, and practicing self-care, you can develop the perseverance necessary to achieve your goals.

Remember that perseverance is not always easy. There will be times when you feel discouraged or overwhelmed. However, by staying committed and reminding yourself of why you started in the first place, you can push through and continue working towards your dreams.

Perseverance is not just about achieving your goals; it is about the journey itself. It is about the personal growth and development that occurs along the way. Embrace the challenges, learn from your mistakes, and keep moving forward. With perseverance, anything is possible.

Chapter 5: The Power of Neurodiversity: How Different Minds Can Change the World

Neurodiversity is a concept that recognizes and celebrates the natural variation in human brain function and behavior. It encompasses the idea that neurological differences, such as autism, dyslexia, and ADHD, are simply variations of the human brain rather than disorders or deficits. This perspective challenges the traditional medical model that pathologizes neurodivergent conditions and instead promotes acceptance and understanding.

Understanding and embracing neurodiversity is crucial for creating a more inclusive society. By recognizing and valuing the unique strengths and perspectives of neurodivergent individuals, we can foster a more equitable and supportive environment for everyone. It is important to move away from a deficit-based approach that focuses on fixing or curing neurodivergent individuals, and instead focus on creating accommodations and support systems that allow them to thrive.

The Science Behind Neurodiversity: Understanding the Brain

Neurodivergent conditions encompass a wide range of neurological differences, including autism, dyslexia, ADHD, and more. These conditions are characterized by differences in brain structure, function, and connectivity. For example, individuals with autism often have atypical patterns of brain development, including differences in the size and connectivity of certain brain regions.

The role of genetics and environment in neurodivergent conditions is complex. While there is evidence to suggest a genetic component to many neurodivergent conditions, it is also clear that environmental factors play a role. For example, exposure to certain toxins during pregnancy has been linked to an increased risk of autism. Additionally, experiences such as trauma or stress can impact brain development and contribute to the manifestation of neurodivergent traits.

Understanding the science behind neurodiversity is important because it helps debunk myths and misconceptions about these conditions. It also highlights the fact that neurodivergent individuals have unique strengths and abilities that should be recognized and celebrated.

The Benefits of Neurodiversity: Different Perspectives and Ideas

Neurodiversity can lead to innovation and creativity. Neurodivergent individuals often have unique ways of thinking and problem-solving that can bring fresh perspectives to a team or project. Their ability to think outside the box and see connections that others may miss can lead to breakthroughs and new ideas.

The importance of diverse perspectives in problem-solving cannot be overstated. When a team is composed of individuals with different ways of thinking, they are more likely to come up with innovative solutions to complex problems. Neurodivergent individuals can offer valuable insights and approaches that may not have been considered by neurotypical individuals.

There are many examples of successful neurodivergent individuals who have made significant contributions in various fields. For instance, Temple Grandin, an autistic woman, has revolutionized the livestock industry with her designs for more humane animal handling systems. Similarly, dyslexic entrepreneur Richard Branson has built a global empire with his innovative ideas and out-of-the-box thinking.

The Challenges of Neurodiversity: Overcoming Stigma and Stereotypes

Despite the benefits of neurodiversity, there are still many stereotypes and misconceptions surrounding neurodivergent individuals. These stereotypes often perpetuate stigma and discrimination, making it difficult for neurodivergent individuals to fully participate in society.

Common stereotypes include the belief that neurodivergent individuals are less intelligent or capable than their neurotypical counterparts. This misconception ignores the fact that neurodivergent individuals often have unique strengths and abilities that can be harnessed in the right environment.

The impact of stigma on neurodivergent individuals can be profound. It can lead to social isolation, low self-esteem, and limited opportunities for education and employment. Many neurodivergent individuals face barriers in accessing support services and accommodations that would enable them to thrive.

Strategies for overcoming stigma and promoting acceptance include education and awareness campaigns that challenge stereotypes and provide accurate information about neurodivergent conditions. It is also important to create inclusive environments that value and accommodate the needs of neurodivergent individuals.

Autism and Neurodiversity: Changing the Narrative

Autism has a complex history and has been viewed in different ways throughout the years. In the past, autism was often seen as a tragic disorder that needed to be cured or fixed. However, the neurodiversity movement has challenged this narrative and promoted a more accepting and inclusive view of autism.

The neurodiversity movement argues that autism is not a disorder to be cured, but rather a natural variation of human brain function. It emphasizes the importance of accepting and accommodating autistic individuals, rather than trying to change them to fit into a neurotypical mold.

Understanding and supporting autistic individuals is crucial for creating an inclusive society. Autistic individuals have unique strengths and abilities that should be recognized and celebrated. By providing appropriate accommodations and support, we can enable autistic individuals to thrive and contribute their unique perspectives to society.

Dyslexia and Neurodiversity: Harnessing Unique Strengths

Dyslexia is a neurodivergent condition characterized by difficulties with reading, writing, and spelling. However, dyslexic individuals often have unique strengths that can be harnessed in certain areas.

Many dyslexic individuals have strong visual-spatial skills, which can be an asset in fields such as design, architecture, or engineering. They may also have excellent problem-solving abilities and creative thinking skills. By recognizing and supporting these strengths, we can help dyslexic individuals excel in their chosen fields.

Strategies for supporting dyslexic individuals in education and the workplace include providing accommodations such as assistive technology or extra time for tasks that involve reading or writing. It is also important to create an environment that values and celebrates diverse ways of learning and communicating.

ADHD and Neurodiversity: Embracing Creativity and Innovation

ADHD is a neurodivergent condition characterized by difficulties with attention, hyperactivity, and impulsivity. While these challenges can be significant, ADHD can also lead to creativity and innovation.

ADHD individuals often have a high level of energy and a tendency to think outside the box. They may have a knack for coming up with new ideas or finding unconventional solutions to problems. By embracing these strengths, we can create environments that foster creativity and innovation.

Strategies for supporting ADHD individuals in education and the workplace include providing structure and clear expectations, as well as allowing for flexibility and movement. It is important to recognize that ADHD individuals may have different ways of learning and processing information, and to provide accommodations that meet their needs.

The Workplace and Neurodiversity: Creating Inclusive Environments

Neurodiversity can bring many benefits to the workplace. Neurodivergent individuals often have unique skills and perspectives that can contribute to innovation and problem-solving. By creating inclusive environments that value and accommodate neurodivergent individuals, companies can tap into this potential.

Strategies for creating inclusive workplaces include providing accommodations such as flexible work schedules or quiet spaces for neurodivergent individuals who may be sensitive to noise or distractions. It is also important to provide training and education for managers and colleagues to increase understanding and awareness of neurodiversity.

There are many examples of companies that have successfully embraced neurodiversity. For instance, software giant Microsoft has a program called Autism Hiring Program that specifically recruits autistic individuals for roles in software development and testing. This program has been highly successful in harnessing the unique strengths of autistic individuals and creating a more inclusive work environment.

Education and Neurodiversity: Supporting All Learners

Accommodating neurodivergent learners is crucial for creating an inclusive education system. Neurodivergent individuals may have different ways of learning and processing information, and it is important to provide accommodations that meet their needs.

Strategies for supporting neurodivergent learners in the classroom include providing visual aids, breaking tasks into smaller steps, and allowing for flexible seating arrangements. It is also important to create a supportive and accepting environment where neurodivergent individuals feel valued and included.

There are many schools and programs that have successfully embraced neurodiversity. For example, the Lab School in Washington, D.C., is a school that specializes in educating students with learning differences. They provide individualized instruction and support to help each student reach their full potential.

Neurodiversity and Social Justice: Advocating for Equality

Neurodiversity intersects with social justice in many ways. The neurodiversity movement advocates for the rights and inclusion of neurodivergent individuals, challenging the discrimination and stigma they often face.

Advocating for neurodivergent individuals' rights involves promoting equal access to education, employment, healthcare, and other essential services. It also involves challenging ableism and promoting acceptance and understanding of neurodiversity in society at large.

There are many social justice movements that have embraced neurodiversity. For example, the disability rights movement has been instrumental in advocating for the rights of neurodivergent individuals and promoting a more inclusive society.

Embracing Neurodiversity for a Better World

Embracing neurodiversity is crucial for creating a more inclusive and innovative society. By recognizing and valuing the unique strengths and perspectives of neurodivergent individuals, we can foster a more equitable and supportive environment for everyone.

Strategies for promoting neurodiversity acceptance and understanding include education and awareness campaigns, creating inclusive environments in education and the workplace, and advocating for the rights of neurodivergent individuals.

By embracing neurodiversity, we can create a world that values and celebrates the diversity of human brains and experiences. This has the potential to not only improve the lives of neurodivergent individuals but also to benefit society as a whole. A neurodiverse world is one that is more inclusive, innovative, and compassionate, and it is a world that we should strive to create for future generations.

Chapter 6: Challenges

Challenges are obstacles or difficulties that we encounter in life. They can come in various forms and can be both external and internal. External challenges may include things like financial problems, relationship issues, or work-related stress, while internal challenges may involve mental and emotional struggles such as anxiety or depression. Challenges are an inevitable part of life, and they play a crucial role in our personal growth and development.

Challenges are important in life because they push us out of our comfort zones and force us to confront our fears and limitations. They provide opportunities for learning, growth, and self-discovery. Without challenges, we would remain stagnant and never reach our full potential. Challenges also help us develop important life skills such as problem-solving, resilience, and perseverance. They teach us valuable lessons about ourselves and the world around us.

The importance of facing challenges in personal growth

Facing challenges is essential for personal growth because it allows us to develop new skills, gain confidence, and expand our horizons. When we step outside of our comfort zones and take on challenges, we are forced to confront our fears and insecurities. This process helps us build resilience and develop a stronger sense of self.

Challenges also provide opportunities for learning and self-discovery. When we face difficult situations, we are forced to think creatively and come up with solutions. This process helps us develop problem-solving skills and enhances our ability to think critically.

Furthermore, facing challenges helps us build confidence. When we overcome obstacles and achieve success, we gain a sense of accomplishment that boosts our self-esteem. This newfound confidence then spills over into other areas of our lives, allowing us to take on even bigger challenges.

The most common types of challenges people face

There are several common types of challenges that people face in their lives. These challenges can vary depending on individual circumstances, but some examples include financial problems, relationship issues, work-related stress, and health problems.

Financial challenges are common and can cause significant stress and anxiety. Many people struggle with debt, living paycheck to paycheck, or not being able to afford basic necessities. These challenges can have a negative impact on mental health and overall well-being.

Relationship issues are another common challenge that people face. Whether it's conflicts with family members, difficulties in romantic relationships, or problems with friends or colleagues, navigating relationships can be challenging and emotionally draining.

Work-related stress is also a common challenge in today's fast-paced and competitive world. Many people experience burnout, high levels of stress, and dissatisfaction with their jobs. Balancing work and personal life can be difficult, leading to challenges in maintaining healthy relationships and overall well-being.

Health problems are another common challenge that people face. Chronic illnesses or disabilities can significantly impact a person's quality of life and present daily challenges. Coping with physical limitations and managing health conditions can be emotionally and physically draining.

Overcoming mental and emotional challenges

Mental and emotional challenges are prevalent in today's society. Anxiety and depression are two of the most common mental health disorders that people face. Overcoming these challenges requires a combination of strategies, including seeking professional help, practicing self-care, and building resilience.

One strategy for overcoming anxiety and depression is seeking therapy or counseling. Talking to a trained professional can provide valuable insights and support in managing these conditions. Therapists can help individuals develop coping mechanisms, challenge negative thought patterns, and provide guidance on self-care practices.

Practicing self-care is another important strategy for overcoming mental and emotional challenges. This includes engaging in activities that promote relaxation, such as exercise, meditation, or spending time in nature. Taking care of one's physical health through proper nutrition, sleep, and regular exercise can also have a positive impact on mental well-being.

Building resilience is crucial for overcoming mental and emotional challenges. Resilience is the ability to bounce back from adversity and adapt to change. Developing resilience involves cultivating a positive mindset, practicing gratitude, and building a support network of friends and family.

Physical challenges and how to overcome them

Physical challenges can be particularly difficult to overcome, especially when they involve chronic illness or disability. Coping with physical limitations requires a combination of strategies, including self-acceptance, seeking support, and finding ways to adapt.

One strategy for coping with chronic illness or disability is self-acceptance. Accepting one's physical limitations and embracing them as part of one's identity can help individuals find peace and contentment. This involves reframing one's perspective and focusing on what can be done rather than what cannot.

Seeking support is another important strategy for overcoming physical challenges. This can involve reaching out to support groups or online communities where individuals facing similar challenges can connect and share experiences. Support from friends, family, or healthcare professionals can also be invaluable in navigating physical challenges.

Finding ways to adapt is crucial for overcoming physical limitations. This may involve making modifications to one's living environment, using assistive devices or technology, or finding alternative ways to engage in activities that were once enjoyed. Adapting may also involve seeking professional help from occupational therapists or physical therapists who can provide guidance on managing physical challenges.

Financial challenges and strategies for overcoming them

Financial challenges are a common source of stress and anxiety for many people. Overcoming these challenges requires a combination of strategies, including budgeting, managing debt, and building financial stability.

One strategy for overcoming financial challenges is creating a budget. This involves tracking income and expenses and making a plan for how money will be allocated. Creating a budget can help individuals gain a better understanding of their financial situation and make informed decisions about spending and saving.

Managing debt is another important strategy for overcoming financial challenges. This may involve consolidating debt, negotiating payment plans with creditors, or seeking professional help from financial advisors. Developing a plan to pay off debt and sticking to it can help individuals regain control of their finances and reduce stress.

Building financial stability is crucial for overcoming financial challenges in the long term. This may involve finding ways to increase income, such as pursuing additional education or training, starting a side business, or seeking higher-paying job opportunities. Building an emergency fund and saving for the future can also provide a sense of security and help individuals navigate unexpected financial challenges.

Challenges in relationships and how to navigate them

Relationship challenges are an inevitable part of life. Whether it's conflicts with family members, difficulties in romantic relationships, or problems with friends or colleagues, navigating relationships can be challenging. Strategies for overcoming relationship challenges include effective communication, conflict resolution skills, and building healthy boundaries.

Effective communication is key to navigating relationship challenges. This involves actively listening to others, expressing oneself clearly and honestly, and being open to feedback. Learning effective communication skills can help individuals express their needs and concerns in a constructive manner and foster healthier relationships.

Conflict resolution skills are also important for navigating relationship challenges. This involves finding common ground, compromising when necessary, and seeking win-win solutions. Learning how to manage conflicts in a respectful and constructive way can help individuals maintain healthy relationships and prevent further damage.

Building healthy boundaries is crucial for navigating relationship challenges. This involves setting limits on what one is willing to accept or tolerate in a relationship and communicating those boundaries clearly to others. Building healthy boundaries helps individuals protect their emotional well-being and maintain healthy relationships based on mutual respect.

Challenges in the workplace and how to cope with them

Workplace challenges are common and can cause significant stress and burnout. Coping with these challenges requires a combination of strategies, including managing stress, setting realistic expectations, and finding work-life balance.

Managing stress is crucial for coping with workplace challenges. This may involve practicing stress management techniques such as deep breathing exercises, mindfulness, or taking regular breaks. Finding healthy ways to cope with stress can help individuals maintain their mental and physical well-being in the workplace.

Setting realistic expectations is another important strategy for coping with workplace challenges. This involves recognizing one's limitations and not taking on more than can be reasonably handled. Setting boundaries and learning to say no when necessary can help individuals avoid burnout and maintain a healthy work-life balance.

Finding work-life balance is crucial for coping with workplace challenges. This involves prioritizing self-care, setting aside time for hobbies and activities outside of work, and maintaining healthy relationships. Finding a balance between work and personal life helps individuals recharge and prevent burnout.

The role of resilience in overcoming challenges

Resilience is the ability to bounce back from adversity and adapt to change. It plays a crucial role in overcoming challenges and is an important skill to develop. Resilience helps individuals navigate difficult situations, maintain a positive mindset, and persevere in the face of obstacles.

Building resilience involves cultivating a positive mindset and reframing negative thoughts. This may involve practicing gratitude, focusing on strengths rather than weaknesses, and seeking out positive experiences. Developing a positive mindset can help individuals maintain optimism and motivation in the face of challenges.

Building a support network is also important for developing resilience. Having a strong support system of friends, family, or mentors can provide emotional support, guidance, and encouragement during challenging times. Seeking support from others can help individuals feel less alone and more capable of overcoming obstacles.

Developing problem-solving skills is another important aspect of building resilience. This involves approaching challenges with a solution-oriented mindset and actively seeking out strategies to overcome obstacles. Developing problem-solving skills helps individuals feel empowered and capable of finding solutions to difficult situations.

Seeking support and resources for overcoming challenges

Seeking help is an important part of overcoming challenges. It's essential to recognize when we need support and reach out to others for assistance. There are various resources available for finding support, including therapy or counseling, support groups, online communities, and helplines.

Therapy or counseling can provide valuable support and guidance in navigating challenges. Mental health professionals can help individuals develop coping mechanisms, challenge negative thought patterns, and provide a safe space for processing emotions. Therapy or counseling can be particularly helpful for overcoming mental and emotional challenges.

Support groups and online communities provide opportunities for individuals facing similar challenges to connect and share experiences. These groups can offer a sense of belonging, validation, and support.

They can also provide valuable insights and strategies for overcoming specific challenges.

Helplines are available for individuals in crisis or in need of immediate support. These helplines are staffed by trained professionals who can provide guidance, resources, and a listening ear. Helplines are particularly useful for individuals experiencing mental health crises or facing urgent challenges.

Celebrating successes and learning from challenges

Celebrating successes is an important part of the journey of overcoming challenges. It's essential to acknowledge and appreciate our achievements, no matter how small they may seem. Celebrating successes boosts self-esteem, reinforces positive behaviors, and provides motivation to continue facing challenges.

Learning from challenges is also crucial for personal growth. Every challenge we face presents an opportunity for learning and self-improvement. Reflecting on the lessons learned from challenges helps us grow stronger, develop new skills, and avoid making the same mistakes in the future.

Conclusion:

Challenges are an inevitable part of life, and they play a crucial role in our personal growth and development. They push us out of our comfort zones, force us to confront our fears and limitations, and provide opportunities for learning, growth, and self-discovery. Challenges come in various forms, including mental and emotional challenges, physical challenges, financial challenges, relationship challenges, and workplace challenges.

Overcoming challenges requires a combination of strategies, including seeking support, developing resilience, and finding ways to adapt. It's important to seek help when needed and utilize the resources available, such as therapy or counseling, support groups, and helplines. Building resilience is crucial for overcoming challenges and involves cultivating a positive mindset, developing problem-solving skills, and building a support network.

It's important to celebrate successes along the way and learn from challenges. Celebrating successes boosts self-esteem and provides motivation to continue facing challenges. Learning from challenges helps us grow stronger, develop new skills, and avoid making the same mistakes in the future. Embracing challenges and using them as opportunities for growth is essential for living a fulfilling and meaningful life.

Chapter 7: From Struggle to Success: Celebrating Triumphs in Life

Life is a journey filled with both triumphs and challenges. It is a rollercoaster ride of ups and downs, twists and turns. However, it is how we handle these challenges that truly define us. The journey to success is often paved with obstacles, but it is important to keep pushing forward, no matter how difficult it may seem.

In order to achieve success, we must be willing to face adversity head-on and overcome the obstacles that come our way. It is through these struggles that we grow and develop as individuals. Each challenge we face provides an opportunity for personal growth and self-discovery.

Overcoming Adversity: Inspiring Stories of Triumph

Throughout history, there have been countless individuals who have faced adversity and triumphed over it. Their stories serve as a source of inspiration and motivation for all of us. One such example is Oprah Winfrey, who overcame a difficult childhood filled with poverty and abuse to become one of the most successful media moguls in the world.

Another inspiring story is that of J.K. Rowling, who went from being a struggling single mother living on welfare to becoming one of the most successful authors of all time with the Harry Potter series. These individuals faced numerous setbacks and challenges along their journey to success, but they never gave up.

What these stories have in common is the resilience and determination displayed by these individuals. They refused to let their circumstances define them and instead used their struggles as fuel to propel them towards success. They believed in themselves and their abilities, even when others doubted them.

The Power of Perseverance: How to Keep Going When the Going Gets Tough

Perseverance is a key trait that separates those who succeed from those who give up. It is the ability to keep going even when faced with seemingly insurmountable obstacles. In order to persevere, it is important to have a clear vision of what you want to achieve and why it is important to you.

During difficult times, it can be helpful to remind yourself of your goals and the reasons why you started on this journey in the first place. Surrounding yourself with positive and supportive people can also provide the encouragement and motivation needed to keep going.

It is also important to take care of yourself both physically and mentally. Engaging in self-care activities such as exercise, meditation, and spending time with loved ones can help reduce stress and increase resilience. Additionally, setting small achievable goals along the way can provide a sense of accomplishment and keep you motivated.

Turning Failure into Success: Lessons Learned from Setbacks

Failure is a natural part of the journey to success. It is through failure that we learn valuable lessons and gain the experience necessary to grow and improve. Many successful individuals have experienced numerous failures before achieving their goals.

Thomas Edison, for example, failed thousands of times before finally inventing the light bulb. He famously said, "I have not failed. I've just found 10,000 ways that won't work." Instead of letting failure discourage him, Edison used it as an opportunity to learn and improve.

The key to turning failure into success is to view it as a learning experience rather than a reflection of your abilities. It is important to analyze what went wrong and identify areas for improvement. By doing so, you can use failure as a stepping stone towards success.

Celebrating Small Wins: Why Every Victory Matters

While it is important to keep our eyes on the ultimate goal, it is equally important to celebrate the small victories along the way. Achieving success is a journey, not a destination, and celebrating each milestone can provide motivation and encouragement.

Celebrating small wins helps to build momentum and confidence. It allows us to acknowledge our progress and reminds us that we are moving in the right direction. By celebrating small victories, we are also more likely to stay motivated and continue working towards our goals.

Additionally, celebrating small wins can help to shift our focus from what we have not yet achieved to what we have accomplished. This positive mindset can increase our overall happiness and satisfaction with our journey to success.

The Role of Mindset in Achieving Success: How to Develop a Winning Attitude

Our mindset plays a crucial role in our ability to achieve success. A positive and growth-oriented mindset can help us overcome challenges and stay motivated during difficult times. Developing a winning attitude starts with believing in yourself and your abilities.

One way to develop a positive mindset is through the practice of gratitude. Taking time each day to reflect on the things you are grateful for can help shift your focus from what is going wrong to what is going right. It can also help you appreciate the progress you have made and the opportunities that lie ahead.

Another important aspect of developing a winning attitude is reframing negative thoughts into positive ones. Instead of dwelling on failures or setbacks, try to see them as opportunities for growth and learning. By reframing negative thoughts, you can maintain a positive outlook and keep moving forward.

Finding Your Passion: Pursuing Your Dreams and Making Them a Reality

Pursuing our passions is essential for a fulfilling and successful life. When we are passionate about something, we are more likely to put in the time and effort required to achieve success. Passion provides us with the motivation and drive needed to overcome obstacles and persevere.

Identifying your passions can be a process of self-discovery. It involves exploring different interests and activities to determine what truly excites and energizes you. Once you have identified your passions, it is important to take action and pursue them.

Taking action towards your passions may involve setting goals, acquiring new skills, or seeking out opportunities that align with your interests. It may also require stepping out of your comfort zone and taking risks. However, the rewards of pursuing your passions far outweigh the challenges.

The Importance of Support Systems: Building a Strong Network of Allies

No one achieves success alone. Building a strong support system is crucial for staying motivated and overcoming challenges. Surrounding yourself with positive and supportive people can provide encouragement, advice, and accountability.

A strong support system can consist of friends, family, mentors, or like-minded individuals who share similar goals and aspirations. These individuals can provide guidance and support during difficult times and celebrate your successes with you.

In addition to building a support system, it is important to seek out mentors who can provide guidance and wisdom based on their own experiences. Mentors can offer valuable insights and help you navigate the challenges that come with pursuing your goals.

Embracing Change: How to Adapt and Thrive in a Changing World

Change is inevitable in life, and it is important to embrace it rather than resist it. Change provides opportunities for growth and new experiences. By embracing change, we can adapt and thrive in a constantly evolving world.

One way to embrace change is by cultivating a growth mindset. A growth mindset is the belief that our abilities can be developed through hard work, dedication, and perseverance. It allows us to see challenges as opportunities for growth rather than obstacles.

Another important aspect of embracing change is being open to new ideas and perspectives. By being open-minded, we can learn from others and gain new insights that can help us navigate change more effectively.

Giving Back: Using Your Success to Make a Positive Impact on Others

Success is not just about personal achievement; it is also about making a positive impact on others. Using our success to give back and help others is not only fulfilling but also creates a ripple effect of positivity in the world.

There are many ways to give back, whether it be through volunteering, mentoring, or donating to causes that are important to you. By using your success to make a positive impact, you can inspire and empower others to achieve their own goals.

Giving back also helps to keep us grounded and grateful for what we have achieved. It reminds us of the importance of using our success for the greater good and encourages us to continue striving for excellence.

Celebrating Your Own Triumphs and

Encouraging Others to Do the Same

In conclusion, life is a journey filled with both struggle and success. It is important to embrace the challenges that come our way and use them as opportunities for growth. By overcoming adversity, celebrating small wins, and developing a positive mindset, we can achieve success and make a positive impact on others.

It is also important to remember that success is not a destination but a journey. Each step along the way is worth celebrating, no matter how small. By celebrating our own triumphs and encouraging others to do the same, we can create a supportive and empowering community that uplifts and inspires one another on our individual journeys to success.

Chapter 8: Breaking Down the Stigma of Diagnosis: Why It's Okay to Seek Help

Addressing the stigma surrounding mental health diagnoses is crucial for creating a society that supports and understands individuals with mental health conditions. Stigma refers to the negative attitudes, beliefs, and stereotypes that surround a particular group of people, in this case, those with mental health diagnoses. This stigma can prevent individuals from seeking help and getting the support they need.

When individuals feel stigmatized, they may be hesitant to reach out for help due to fear of judgment or discrimination. This can have serious consequences for their mental health and well-being. By breaking down the stigma surrounding mental health diagnoses, we can create an environment where individuals feel safe and supported in seeking the help they need.

Understanding the Stigma of Diagnosis: Its Origins and Effects

Stigma is a deeply ingrained societal issue that has its roots in historical and cultural beliefs about mental health. In many cultures, mental illness has been viewed as a sign of weakness or moral failing, leading to shame and discrimination against those who experience it. These negative beliefs have perpetuated the stigma surrounding mental health diagnoses.

The effects of stigma on individuals with mental health diagnoses are far-reaching. Stigma can lead to feelings of shame, isolation, and low self-esteem. It can also prevent individuals from seeking help and accessing appropriate treatment. This can result in worsening symptoms, decreased quality of life, and even increased risk of suicide.

The Harmful Effects of Stigma: How It Prevents People from Seeking Help

Stigma surrounding mental health diagnoses can have a significant impact on an individual's willingness to seek help. The fear of being judged or labeled as "crazy" or "weak" can be a powerful deterrent. Many individuals may also internalize these negative beliefs about themselves, leading to feelings of shame and self-blame.

Additionally, stigma can create barriers to accessing appropriate treatment and support. Individuals may be hesitant to disclose their mental health diagnoses to healthcare providers, fearing that they will be treated differently or not taken seriously. This can result in delayed or inadequate treatment, further exacerbating their symptoms and impairing their ability to function.

The Importance of Seeking Help: Why It Can Be Life-Changing

Seeking help and receiving a diagnosis can be a life-changing step for individuals with mental health conditions. It can provide validation for their experiences and help them understand that they are not alone. A diagnosis can also open the door to appropriate treatment and support, leading to improved mental health outcomes and a better quality of life.

Receiving a diagnosis allows individuals to gain a better understanding of their condition and how it affects them. This knowledge can empower them to take control of their mental health and make informed decisions about their treatment options. It can also help them communicate their needs more effectively to healthcare providers and loved ones.

The Benefits of Diagnosis: Understanding Your Condition and How to Manage It

One of the key benefits of receiving a diagnosis is gaining a better understanding of your condition. A diagnosis provides a framework for understanding your symptoms, their causes, and potential treatment options. This knowledge can help individuals make sense of their experiences and develop strategies for managing their condition.

A diagnosis also allows individuals to access more targeted and effective treatment options. With a clear understanding of their condition, healthcare providers can develop personalized treatment plans that address the specific needs of the individual. This can lead to improved symptom management, increased functioning, and an overall better quality of life.

Overcoming the Fear of Diagnosis: How to Take the First Step

Many individuals may have fears and concerns about seeking a diagnosis for their mental health condition. They may worry about being labeled or stigmatized, or they may fear what the diagnosis might mean for their future. Overcoming these fears is an important step towards seeking help and breaking down the stigma surrounding mental health diagnoses.

One strategy for overcoming the fear of diagnosis is to educate yourself about mental health conditions and the diagnostic process. Understanding that mental health conditions are common and treatable can help alleviate some of the fear and stigma associated with them. It can also be helpful to seek support from trusted friends, family members, or mental health professionals who can provide guidance and reassurance.

The Role of Mental Health Professionals: How

They Can Help You

Mental health professionals play a crucial role in the diagnosis and treatment process. They have the knowledge and expertise to accurately assess and diagnose mental health conditions. They can also provide support and guidance throughout the diagnosis process, helping individuals understand their condition and develop a treatment plan.

Mental health professionals can also provide ongoing support and therapy to individuals with mental health diagnoses. Therapy can help individuals develop coping strategies, improve their emotional well-being, and enhance their overall quality of life. By working with a mental health professional, individuals can receive the support they need to manage their condition effectively.

The Importance of Support: Finding a Community That Understands You

Finding a supportive community that understands your experiences is crucial for breaking down the stigma surrounding mental health diagnoses. Connecting with others who have similar experiences can provide validation, support, and a sense of belonging. It can also help individuals feel less alone in their journey towards better mental health.

There are many ways to find support, both online and offline. Support groups, either in-person or virtual, can provide a safe space for individuals to share their experiences and learn from others. Online forums and social media groups can also be valuable resources for connecting with others who have similar experiences.

The Power of Self-Care: How to Take Care of Yourself During the Diagnosis Process

Self-care is an essential component of managing your mental health, especially during the diagnosis process. Taking care of yourself physically, emotionally, and mentally can help reduce stress, improve your overall well-being, and enhance your ability to cope with the challenges that come with seeking a diagnosis.

Practicing self-care can look different for everyone, but some common strategies include getting enough sleep, eating a balanced diet, engaging in regular physical activity, and engaging in activities that bring you joy and relaxation. It's also important to prioritize self-compassion and give yourself permission to take breaks and rest when needed.

Breaking Down the Stigma: How to Educate Others and Advocate for Change

Breaking down the stigma surrounding mental health diagnoses requires education and advocacy. By educating others about mental health conditions and challenging stereotypes and misconceptions, we can help create a more understanding and supportive society.

One way to educate others is by sharing your own experiences with mental health diagnoses. By speaking openly about your journey, you can help reduce stigma and encourage others to seek help. It's also important to challenge negative beliefs and stereotypes when you encounter them, whether it's in conversations with friends and family or in public forums.

Why Seeking Help is a Brave and Important Step in Your Journey

Seeking help for a mental health condition is a brave and important step towards better mental health and well-being. By breaking down the stigma surrounding mental health diagnoses, we can create a society that supports and understands individuals with mental health conditions. Remember that you are not alone in your journey, and there are resources and support available to help you along the way.

Chapter 9: Growing Up Too Fast: The Impact of Technology on Childhood Development

In today's digital age, technology has become an integral part of children's lives. From smartphones and tablets to video games and social media, technology is everywhere. This prevalence of technology has undoubtedly had a significant impact on childhood development. While there are many benefits to technology use, there are also negative effects that need to be considered.

The Role of Technology in Accelerating Childhood Development

One of the most significant benefits of technology in childhood development is its role in education and learning. With the internet at their fingertips, children have access to a wealth of information that can enhance their knowledge and understanding of various subjects. Educational apps and online resources can make learning fun and engaging, allowing children to develop new skills and expand their horizons.

Technology also plays a crucial role in enhancing creativity and imagination. With tools like digital art programs and music production software, children can explore their artistic talents and express themselves in new and exciting ways. Additionally, video games can foster problem-solving skills and critical thinking as children navigate through virtual worlds and overcome challenges.

The Negative Effects of Technology on Childhood Development

While technology can be beneficial, excessive screen time can have negative effects on cognitive development. Research has shown that too much screen time can lead to decreased attention span, poor memory, and difficulty with problem-solving skills. This is because excessive screen time can overstimulate the brain and hinder its ability to focus and concentrate.

Furthermore, technology can also impact language and communication skills. With the rise of texting and social media, children may rely more on written communication rather than face-to-face interactions. This can lead to a decrease in verbal communication skills, as well as a lack of understanding of nonverbal cues such as body language and facial expressions.

The Impact of Social Media on Children's Self-Image and Identity

Social media has become a significant influence on children's self-esteem and body image. With platforms like Instagram and Snapchat, children are constantly exposed to carefully curated images of their peers, celebrities, and influencers. This can lead to feelings of inadequacy and a distorted perception of beauty and success.

Additionally, social media plays a role in shaping children's identity. With the ability to create online personas and present themselves in a certain way, children may feel pressure to conform to societal expectations or portray an idealized version of themselves. This can lead to a lack of authenticity and a disconnect between their online and offline selves.

The Link Between Technology and Attention Deficit Disorder

There is a growing concern about the link between technology use and Attention Deficit Disorder (ADHD) symptoms in children. Research has shown that excessive screen time can contribute to attention difficulties, impulsivity, and hyperactivity. This is because technology provides constant stimulation and instant gratification, making it difficult for children with ADHD to focus on tasks that require sustained attention.

Furthermore, technology can also impact children's ability to focus and concentrate. With the constant distractions of notifications, videos, and games, it can be challenging for children to stay focused on one task for an extended period. This can hinder their ability to complete homework assignments or engage in activities that require sustained attention.

The Rise of Cyberbullying and Its Effects on Children's Mental Health

With the rise of technology, cyberbullying has become a prevalent issue among children. Cyberbullying refers to the use of technology to harass, intimidate, or humiliate others. This can have severe consequences for children's mental health and well-being.

Research has shown that cyberbullying can lead to increased levels of anxiety, depression, and low self-esteem in victims. It can also contribute to feelings of isolation and social withdrawal. Additionally, cyberbullying can have long-lasting effects on mental health, with some victims experiencing symptoms of post-traumatic stress disorder (PTSD).

The Relationship Between Technology and Sleep Deprivation in Children

The use of technology, particularly before bedtime, can have a significant impact on children's sleep patterns. The blue light emitted by screens can interfere with the production of melatonin, a hormone that regulates sleep. This can make it difficult for children to fall asleep and stay asleep, leading to sleep deprivation.

Sleep is crucial for childhood development, as it plays a vital role in memory consolidation, learning, and overall well-being. Lack of sleep can lead to difficulties with attention, concentration, and academic performance. It can also contribute to mood swings, irritability, and behavioral problems.

The Impact of Screen Time on Children's Physical Health and Well-Being

Excessive screen time has been linked to an increased risk of obesity in children. This is because sedentary activities such as watching TV or playing video games often involve sitting for long periods and snacking on unhealthy foods. Additionally, excessive screen time can lead to a decrease in physical activity levels as children spend less time engaging in active play or sports.

Obesity can have serious health consequences for children, including an increased risk of chronic conditions such as diabetes, heart disease, and certain types of cancer. It can also contribute to low self-esteem and body image issues.

The Importance of Developing Real-Life Social Skills in the Age of Social Media

While technology provides opportunities for social connection, it is essential for children to develop real-life social skills through face-to-face interactions. These skills include empathy, active listening, conflict resolution, and the ability to read nonverbal cues.

Social media can impact social skills and relationships by promoting superficial connections and reducing the need for face-to-face interactions. Children may rely on likes and comments for validation rather than developing meaningful relationships based on shared interests and values.

Balancing Technology Use with Other Activities for Optimal Childhood Development

To promote healthy childhood development, it is crucial to find a balance between technology use and other activities. This can be achieved by setting limits on screen time and encouraging children to engage in a variety of activities such as outdoor play, reading, arts and crafts, and sports.

Parents and caregivers can implement strategies such as creating technology-free zones or designated screen time hours. It is also important to model healthy technology use by limiting their own screen time and engaging in activities that promote face-to-face interactions.

Navigating the Digital World to Promote Healthy Childhood Development

In conclusion, the prevalence of technology in children's lives has undoubtedly changed the landscape of childhood in the digital age. While there are many benefits to technology use, there are also negative effects that need to be considered. It is essential for parents and caregivers to monitor technology use and promote a healthy balance between technology use and other activities for optimal childhood development. By navigating the digital world responsibly, we can ensure that children grow up with the skills and abilities they need to thrive in an increasingly digital society.

Chapter 10: Adolescence

Adolescence is a period of significant growth and change that occurs between childhood and adulthood. It is a time when individuals experience physical, emotional, cognitive, and social changes that shape their development and identity. Understanding adolescence is crucial for parents, caregivers, and educators as it allows them to provide the necessary support and guidance during this transitional period.

The Physical Changes of Adolescence

A. Puberty

Puberty is the process of sexual maturation that marks the beginning of adolescence. It involves the development of secondary sexual characteristics such as breast development in girls and facial hair growth in boys. Hormonal changes during puberty also lead to the onset of menstruation in girls and the production of sperm in boys. These physical changes can be both exciting and confusing for adolescents as they navigate their new bodies.

B. Growth Spurts

Adolescence is also characterized by rapid growth spurts. During this time, individuals experience a significant increase in height and weight as their bodies prepare for adulthood. This growth can sometimes be uneven, with certain body parts growing at different rates, leading to temporary awkwardness or clumsiness. It is important for adolescents to understand that these changes are normal and temporary.

C. Changes in Body Composition

In addition to growth spurts, adolescents also experience changes in body composition. Boys tend to gain more muscle mass, while girls develop more body fat. These changes are influenced by hormonal fluctuations and can impact self-esteem and body image. It is important for adolescents to maintain a healthy lifestyle through proper nutrition and exercise during this time.

The Emotional Changes of Adolescence

A. Mood Swings

One of the most well-known aspects of adolescence is the presence of mood swings. Hormonal changes during this time can lead to increased emotional volatility, with adolescents experiencing intense highs and lows. These mood swings can be challenging for both the individual and those around them, but it is important to remember that they are a normal part of adolescent development.

B. Increased Emotional Intensity

Along with mood swings, adolescents also experience increased emotional intensity. They may feel emotions more deeply and have difficulty regulating their emotions. This can lead to heightened sensitivity and a tendency to overreact to situations. It is important for adults to provide a supportive and understanding environment for adolescents during this time.

C. Developing Self-Concept

Adolescence is a period of self-discovery and identity formation. During this time, individuals begin to develop a sense of self and explore their personal values, beliefs, and interests. This process can be challenging as adolescents navigate societal expectations and peer influences. It is important for adults to encourage self-expression and provide opportunities for adolescents to explore their interests and passions.

The Cognitive Changes of Adolescence

A. Increased Abstract Thinking

One of the key cognitive changes that occur during adolescence is the development of abstract thinking skills. Adolescents begin to think more hypothetically and consider multiple perspectives on a given issue. This allows them to engage in more complex problem-solving and critical thinking.

B. Developing Decision-Making Skills

As adolescents gain the ability to think abstractly, they also begin to develop their decision-making skills. They become more capable of weighing the pros and cons of different options and considering the potential consequences of their actions. However, this newfound ability can also lead to risk-taking behavior as adolescents test boundaries and explore their independence.

C. Developing Critical Thinking Skills

In addition to abstract thinking and decision-making skills, adolescence is also a time when individuals develop critical thinking skills. They learn to question information, evaluate evidence, and form their own opinions. This is an important skill for navigating the complex world around them and making informed decisions.

The Social Changes of Adolescence

A. Increased Importance of Peer Relationships

During adolescence, peer relationships become increasingly important. Adolescents seek validation and acceptance from their peers and may prioritize their opinions over those of adults. Peer relationships provide a sense of belonging and identity, but they can also influence behavior and decision-making.

B. Developing Romantic Relationships

Adolescence is also a time when individuals begin to explore romantic relationships. They experience their first crushes, go on dates, and navigate the complexities of romantic attraction. These relationships can be both exciting and challenging as adolescents learn about intimacy, trust, and communication.

C. Increased Independence from Parents

As adolescents develop their own identities and seek autonomy, they naturally begin to assert their independence from their parents. They may challenge authority, question rules, and seek more freedom. This can be a difficult transition for parents, but it is important to provide guidance and support while allowing adolescents to develop their own sense of responsibility.

The Importance of Identity Development in Adolescence

A. Developing a Sense of Self

Identity development is a central task of adolescence. It involves exploring one's values, beliefs, interests, and goals in order to form a coherent sense of self. This process can be challenging as adolescents navigate societal expectations and peer influences. It is important for adults to provide a supportive environment that allows for self-expression and exploration.

B. Exploring Personal Values and Beliefs

Adolescence is a time when individuals begin to question the values and beliefs they have inherited from their families and society. They may experiment with different ideologies and philosophies as they search for meaning and purpose. It is important for adults to encourage open-mindedness and provide opportunities for adolescents to explore different perspectives.

C. Developing a Positive Self-Image

Positive self-image is crucial for healthy adolescent development. Adolescents who have a positive self-image are more likely to have higher self-esteem, better mental health, and stronger relationships. It is important for adults to provide positive reinforcement, celebrate achievements, and help adolescents develop a realistic and healthy view of themselves.

The Role of Peer Relationships in Adolescence

A. Peer Pressure

Peer pressure is a common aspect of adolescence. Adolescents may feel pressure to conform to the norms and expectations of their peer group, even if it goes against their own values or beliefs. It is important for adults to educate adolescents about the potential risks of peer pressure and provide strategies for resisting negative influences.

B. Positive Peer Influence

While peer pressure can be negative, peer relationships can also have a positive influence on adolescents. Positive peer relationships can provide support, encouragement, and a sense of belonging. They can also serve as role models and help adolescents develop social skills and empathy.

C. Developing Social Skills

Adolescence is a critical time for developing social skills. Adolescents learn how to navigate social situations, communicate effectively, and build meaningful relationships. It is important for adults to provide opportunities for adolescents to practice these skills and provide guidance and feedback when needed.

The Impact of Technology on Adolescence

A. Social Media

The rise of social media has had a significant impact on adolescence. It has changed the way adolescents communicate, form relationships, and present themselves to the world. While social media can provide opportunities for connection and self-expression, it can also contribute to feelings of inadequacy, cyberbullying, and addiction.

B. Video Games

Video games have become increasingly popular among adolescents, with many spending hours each day playing them. While video games can be a source of entertainment and relaxation, excessive gaming can lead to social isolation, poor academic performance, and addiction. It is important for adults to set limits and encourage a healthy balance between gaming and other activities.

C. Internet Addiction

Internet addiction is a growing concern among adolescents. Excessive use of the internet can interfere with schoolwork, relationships, and overall well-being. It is important for adults to monitor internet use and provide guidance on healthy online behaviors.

The Risks and Challenges of Adolescence

A. Substance Abuse

Adolescence is a time when individuals may experiment with drugs and alcohol. Peer pressure, curiosity, and a desire for independence can contribute to substance abuse. It is important for adults to educate adolescents about the risks of substance abuse and provide support and resources for prevention and intervention.

B. Mental Health Issues

Adolescence is also a time when mental health issues may emerge or worsen. Hormonal changes, academic stress, peer pressure, and identity development can all contribute to anxiety, depression, and other mental health disorders. It is important for adults to be aware of the signs of mental health issues and provide access to appropriate support and treatment.

C. Risky Behaviors

Adolescents are more likely to engage in risky behaviors such as unprotected sex, reckless driving, and substance abuse. These behaviors can have serious consequences for their physical and emotional well-being. It is important for adults to provide education on risk prevention and encourage responsible decision-making.

Supporting Adolescents Through the Transition to Adulthood

A. Positive Parenting Strategies

Parents play a crucial role in supporting adolescents through the transition to adulthood. Positive parenting strategies such as open communication, setting clear boundaries, and providing emotional support can help adolescents navigate the challenges of adolescence.

B. Encouraging Healthy Habits

Adolescence is a critical time for establishing healthy habits that will carry into adulthood. Adults can encourage adolescents to prioritize their physical and mental health by promoting regular exercise, healthy eating, adequate sleep, and stress management techniques.

C. Seeking Professional Help

In some cases, adolescents may require professional help to navigate the challenges of adolescence. Mental health professionals, counselors, and therapists can provide support, guidance, and intervention when needed. It is important for adults to be aware of available resources and seek help when necessary.

Resources for Parents and Caregivers of Adolescents

A. Books and Websites

There are numerous books and websites available that provide information and guidance on parenting adolescents. These resources can offer insights into adolescent development, strategies for communication and discipline, and tips for supporting mental health and well-being.

B. Support Groups

Support groups for parents and caregivers of adolescents can provide a valuable source of support and understanding. These groups allow individuals to share their experiences, learn from others, and gain perspective on the challenges of parenting during adolescence.

C. Counseling Services

Counseling services can be beneficial for both adolescents and their parents or caregivers. Individual counseling can help adolescents navigate the challenges of adolescence, while family counseling can improve communication and strengthen relationships.

Understanding adolescence is crucial for parents, caregivers, and educators as it allows them to provide the necessary support and guidance during this transitional period. Adolescence is a time of significant physical, emotional, cognitive, and social changes that shape an individual's development and identity. By recognizing the unique challenges and opportunities of adolescence, adults can help adolescents navigate this transformative period with confidence and resilience.

Chapter 11: Redefining Family: Exploring the Modern Definition of What it Means to be a Family

Family dynamics have undergone significant changes in recent years, reflecting the evolving nature of society. Traditional family structures, such as the nuclear family, are no longer the only prevalent form of family. Blended families, chosen families, same-sex parenting, single parenthood, multigenerational households, foster families, adoption, co-parenting, and virtual families are just a few examples of the diverse family structures that exist today. Each of these structures brings its own unique set of benefits and challenges, reshaping our understanding of what it means to be a family.

The Evolution of Family Structures: From Nuclear to Blended Families

The nuclear family, consisting of a married couple and their biological children, has long been considered the ideal family structure in many societies. This structure was particularly prevalent in the post-World War II era when traditional gender roles were reinforced and families were seen as stable units. However, with changing social norms and an increase in divorce rates, the rise of blended families has become more common.

Blended families are formed when two individuals with children from previous relationships come together to form a new family unit. This can create a complex dynamic as children adjust to new siblings and step-parents. The impact on family dynamics can be both positive and challenging. On one hand, blended families provide an opportunity for individuals to create new bonds and expand their support networks. On the other hand, conflicts may arise as individuals navigate their roles within the new family structure.

Beyond Blood Ties: The Rise of Chosen Families

Chosen families are formed by individuals who are not related by blood or marriage but have chosen to create a familial bond with one another. This can include close friends or members of the LGBTQ+ community who may have been rejected by their biological families. Chosen families provide a sense of belonging and support for individuals who may not have strong ties to their biological families.

The rise of chosen families can be attributed to various factors, including changing societal attitudes towards non-traditional family structures and the increasing acceptance of diverse identities. Chosen families offer a sense of belonging and support that may not be present in biological families. However, there can also be challenges in navigating these relationships, as individuals may have different expectations and boundaries.

Same-Sex Parenting: Redefining Traditional Gender Roles in Families

Same-sex parenting refers to couples of the same gender raising children together. This form of parenting challenges traditional gender roles within families, as it does not adhere to the traditional model of a mother and father. Same-sex parents often face legal and social challenges, including discrimination and lack of recognition.

Despite these challenges, same-sex parenting has been shown to have positive effects on children's well-being. Research has consistently shown that children raised by same-sex parents fare just as well as those raised by opposite-sex parents. Same-sex parenting also provides an opportunity to challenge traditional gender roles and promote gender equality within families.

Single Parenthood: The Growing Trend of Solo Parenting

Single parenthood is on the rise globally, with more individuals choosing to become parents on their own or becoming single parents due to divorce or separation. Single parents face unique challenges, including financial strain, lack of support, and balancing work and parenting responsibilities.

Support systems for single parents are crucial in ensuring their well-being and the well-being of their children. These support systems can include access to affordable childcare, flexible work arrangements, and community resources. Additionally, single parents can benefit from joining support groups or seeking counseling to navigate the challenges they face.

Multigenerational Households: The Benefits and Challenges of Living with Extended Family

Multigenerational households are characterized by multiple generations living under one roof. This can include grandparents, parents, and children living together in a shared space. Multigenerational households have become more common in recent years due to economic factors, cultural norms, and the desire for intergenerational support.

Living with extended family can provide numerous benefits, including shared expenses, emotional support, and the passing down of cultural traditions and values. However, there can also be challenges in terms of privacy, conflicting expectations, and generational differences. Open communication and mutual respect are essential in maintaining a harmonious living arrangement.

Foster Families: Providing a Safe Haven for Children in Need

Foster families play a crucial role in providing temporary care for children who are unable to live with their biological families. These children may have experienced abuse, neglect, or other forms of trauma. Foster families provide a safe and nurturing environment for these children while they await reunification with their biological families or find permanent placements through adoption.

Being a foster parent comes with its own set of challenges and rewards. Foster parents must navigate the complexities of the child welfare system, work with birth parents, and provide stability and support to children who may have experienced trauma. Despite the challenges, foster parents have the opportunity to make a positive impact on the lives of vulnerable children.

Adoption: Creating Forever Families Through Legal Means

Adoption is the legal process by which individuals or couples become the legal parents of a child who is not biologically their own. There are various types of adoption, including domestic adoption, international adoption, and foster care adoption. Adoption provides individuals or couples with the opportunity to create a forever family and give a child a loving and stable home.

The process of adoption can be both legally and emotionally complex. Prospective adoptive parents must navigate legal requirements, undergo home studies, and often wait for an extended period before being matched with a child. Emotionally, adoption involves navigating issues of identity, loss, and attachment for both the adoptive parents and the child. However, the rewards of adoption are immeasurable as families are formed and lives are forever changed.

Co-Parenting: Sharing Parenting Responsibilities with Non-Romantic Partners

Co-parenting refers to the shared parenting responsibilities between two individuals who are not in a romantic relationship. This can include friends, siblings, or even strangers who have chosen to raise a child together. Co-parenting can be a viable option for individuals who want to become parents but do not wish to enter into a romantic relationship or who are unable to have children biologically.

Co-parenting offers numerous benefits, including shared financial responsibilities, emotional support, and the opportunity for a child to have multiple parental figures. However, co-parenting also comes with its own set of challenges, including communication and decision-making conflicts. Clear boundaries and open communication are essential in maintaining a healthy co-parenting relationship.

The Impact of Technology on Family Dynamics: Virtual Families and Online Communities

Technology has had a profound impact on family dynamics, with the rise of virtual families and online communities. Virtual families refer to individuals who form familial bonds through online platforms or video games. Online communities provide support and connection for individuals who may not have access to traditional support networks.

The benefits of technology in family dynamics include increased communication and connection, access to information and resources, and the ability to connect with individuals from diverse backgrounds. However, there can also be challenges, such as the potential for addiction or the erosion of face-to-face interactions. It is important for families to strike a balance between utilizing technology for positive purposes while also maintaining healthy relationships offline.

Celebrating Diversity: Embracing Different

Family Structures and Cultures

Embracing diversity in family structures and cultures is crucial in creating inclusive and accepting societies. Different family structures, such as blended families, chosen families, same-sex parents, single parents, multigenerational households, foster families, adoptive families, and co-parenting arrangements, all contribute to the rich tapestry of human experience.

By celebrating diversity, we can challenge societal norms and expectations, promote equality and acceptance, and create a sense of belonging for all individuals. Embracing different family structures and cultures allows us to learn from one another, broaden our perspectives, and foster empathy and understanding.

The landscape of family dynamics has evolved significantly in recent years, reflecting the changing nature of society. Traditional family structures are no longer the only prevalent form of family, with blended families, chosen families, same-sex parenting, single parenthood, multigenerational households, foster families, adoption, co-parenting, and virtual families becoming more common. Each of these structures brings its own unique set of benefits and challenges, reshaping our understanding of what it means to be a family. It is important to understand and accept different family structures and cultures in order to create inclusive and accepting societies that celebrate diversity.

Chapter 12: The Power of Support: How It Can Change Your Life

Support is a fundamental aspect of human life that plays a crucial role in our overall well-being and success. It can be defined as the assistance, encouragement, or comfort provided to someone during challenging times or in pursuit of their goals. Support can come in various forms, including emotional, physical, financial, social, and professional. Each type of support has its own unique impact on our lives, helping us navigate difficulties, achieve our goals, build strong relationships, and ultimately lead a fulfilling life.

The Different Types of Support and How They Impact Your Life

a) Emotional support: Emotional support refers to the empathy, understanding, and encouragement provided by others during times of emotional distress or difficulty. It can come from friends, family members, partners, or even therapists. Emotional support helps individuals feel validated and understood, reducing feelings of loneliness and isolation. It provides a safe space for individuals to express their emotions and seek guidance or advice.

b) Physical support: Physical support involves the tangible assistance provided by others to meet our physical needs. This can include help with daily tasks such as cooking, cleaning, or running errands. Physical support is particularly important for individuals with physical disabilities or health conditions that limit their mobility. It allows them to maintain their independence and quality of life.

c) Financial support: Financial support refers to the monetary assistance provided by others to meet our financial needs or achieve specific goals. This can include financial contributions from family members, scholarships, grants, or loans. Financial support can have a significant impact on an individual's life by providing them with the resources necessary to pursue education, start a business, or overcome financial hardships.

d) Social support: Social support involves the network of relationships we have with others that provide us with a sense of belonging and connection. It includes friends, family members, colleagues, and community groups. Social support plays a crucial role in our mental and emotional well-being, providing us with a support system to lean on during challenging times and celebrate our successes.

e) Professional support: Professional support refers to the guidance, mentorship, and resources provided by experts in a specific field to help individuals achieve their professional goals. This can include career coaches, mentors, or professional organizations. Professional support can provide individuals with valuable insights, advice, and opportunities that can accelerate their career growth and success.

How Emotional Support Can Help You Overcome Difficult Times

Emotional support is a vital form of support that can help individuals navigate difficult times and overcome emotional challenges. It involves providing empathy, understanding, and encouragement to someone who is experiencing emotional distress. Emotional support can come in various forms, such as listening without judgment, offering comforting words, or simply being present for someone in need.

During difficult times, emotional support can make a significant difference in an individual's ability to cope and recover. It provides a sense of validation and understanding, reducing feelings of loneliness and isolation. Knowing that someone is there for you and cares about your well-being can provide a much-needed source of comfort and strength.

For example, imagine someone going through a breakup. They may feel overwhelmed with sadness, anger, or confusion. Emotional support from friends or family members can help them process their emotions, gain perspective on the situation, and find the strength to move forward. By providing a listening ear, offering words of encouragement, or even just being physically present, emotional support can help individuals navigate the complexities of their emotions and find healing.

The Role of Physical Support in Achieving Your Goals

Physical support plays a crucial role in helping individuals achieve their goals by providing the necessary assistance to meet their physical needs. It involves tangible actions taken by others to help someone accomplish tasks or overcome physical limitations.

Examples of physical support include helping someone with disabilities navigate their environment, assisting with household chores or errands, or providing transportation to appointments or events. Physical support allows individuals to maintain their independence and quality of life, even in the face of physical challenges.

For instance, consider someone recovering from surgery. They may have limited mobility and require assistance with daily tasks such as cooking, cleaning, or bathing. Physical support from friends or family members can help them navigate these challenges and focus on their recovery. By providing practical assistance, physical support enables individuals to continue pursuing their goals and maintain a sense of normalcy in their lives.

How Financial Support Can Change Your Life for the Better

Financial support can have a transformative impact on an individual's life by providing them with the resources necessary to pursue their goals and overcome financial hardships. It involves monetary assistance provided by others, such as family members, scholarships, grants, or loans.

Financial support can come in various forms, depending on the specific needs and goals of the individual. It can include funding for education, starting a business, purchasing a home, or covering basic living expenses during times of financial difficulty.

For example, imagine someone who dreams of pursuing higher education but lacks the financial means to do so. Financial support in the form of scholarships or grants can make their dreams a reality by providing them with the necessary funds to enroll in a university or college. This financial support not only opens doors for educational opportunities but also enhances their future career prospects and overall quality of life.

The Power of Social Support in Building Strong Relationships

Social support plays a vital role in building strong relationships and fostering a sense of belonging and connection. It involves the network of relationships we have with others that provide us with emotional, practical, and informational support.

Examples of social support include spending time with friends or family members, participating in community activities or groups, or seeking advice from trusted individuals. Social support provides us with a sense of validation, understanding, and companionship that is essential for our mental and emotional well-being.

For instance, imagine someone going through a difficult time in their personal life, such as the loss of a loved one or a major life transition. Social support from friends or family members can provide them with a safe space to express their emotions, seek guidance or advice, and find comfort in the presence of others. By offering empathy, understanding, and companionship, social support helps individuals navigate challenging times and build resilience.

The Benefits of Professional Support in Achieving Success

Professional support plays a crucial role in helping individuals achieve success in their chosen fields by providing guidance, mentorship, and resources. It involves seeking assistance from experts or professionals who have the knowledge and experience to help individuals navigate their career paths and achieve their professional goals.

Examples of professional support include career coaches, mentors, or professional organizations. Professional support can provide individuals with valuable insights, advice, and opportunities that can accelerate their career growth and success.

For example, imagine someone starting a new business. They may lack the necessary knowledge or experience to navigate the complexities of entrepreneurship. Professional support from mentors or business coaches can provide them with guidance on business strategies, marketing techniques, or financial management. This professional support not only helps individuals avoid common pitfalls but also enhances their chances of success in their chosen field.

How Support Groups Can Help You Overcome Personal Challenges

Support groups are a valuable resource for individuals facing personal challenges or seeking personal growth. They involve a gathering of individuals who share similar experiences, providing each other with empathy, understanding, and encouragement.

Support groups can be found for various topics or issues, such as addiction recovery, grief support, mental health, or parenting. They provide a safe space for individuals to share their experiences, learn from others facing similar challenges, and gain valuable insights and coping strategies.

For instance, imagine someone struggling with addiction. Joining a support group for addiction recovery can provide them with a community of individuals who understand their struggles and can offer guidance and support. By sharing their experiences, listening to others, and receiving encouragement, support groups can help individuals overcome personal challenges and find the strength to make positive changes in their lives.

The Importance of Self-Support in Achieving Personal Growth

Self-support is an essential aspect of achieving personal growth and well-being. It involves taking care of oneself, both physically and emotionally, and developing self-compassion, self-confidence, and self-care practices.

Examples of self-support include engaging in regular exercise, practicing mindfulness or meditation, setting boundaries, seeking therapy or counseling, or pursuing hobbies and interests that bring joy and fulfillment.

Self-support is crucial because it allows individuals to take ownership of their well-being and actively contribute to their personal growth. It helps individuals develop resilience, self-awareness, and the ability to navigate life's challenges with grace and strength.

For example, imagine someone experiencing high levels of stress or burnout due to work or personal responsibilities. Self-support practices such as setting boundaries, practicing self-care, or seeking therapy can help them manage their stress levels, prioritize their well-being, and achieve a healthier work-life balance. By investing in self-support, individuals can cultivate a strong foundation for personal growth and overall well-being.

Overcoming Barriers to Receiving Support and Asking for Help

While support is essential for our well-being and success, there are often barriers that prevent us from seeking or receiving the support we need. Common barriers include fear of judgment or vulnerability, cultural or societal expectations, lack of awareness or resources, or a belief in self-reliance.

To overcome these barriers, it is important to recognize that asking for help is not a sign of weakness but rather a sign of strength. It takes courage to acknowledge our limitations and reach out for support. It is also important to challenge societal norms that promote self-reliance and instead embrace the power of community and connection.

Additionally, seeking support from trusted individuals or professionals can provide a safe space to share our struggles and receive guidance or assistance. Building a support network of individuals who understand and support our goals can also help overcome barriers and create a supportive environment.

Embracing the Power of Support for a Fulfilling Life

In conclusion, support is a fundamental aspect of human life that plays a crucial role in our overall well-being and success. It comes in various forms, including emotional, physical, financial, social, and professional support. Each type of support has its own unique impact on our lives, helping us navigate difficulties, achieve our goals, build strong relationships, and ultimately lead a fulfilling life.

Emotional support provides empathy, understanding, and encouragement during difficult times. Physical support helps individuals meet their physical needs and maintain their independence. Financial support provides the resources necessary to pursue goals and overcome financial hardships. Social support fosters a sense of belonging and connection. Professional support offers guidance and resources to achieve success in one's chosen field. Support groups provide a community of individuals facing similar challenges. Self-support allows individuals to take ownership of their well-being and personal growth.

While there may be barriers to seeking or receiving support, it is important to overcome these barriers and embrace the power of community and connection. Asking for help is not a sign of weakness but rather a sign of strength. By seeking and embracing support in life, we can navigate challenges with resilience, achieve our goals with confidence, build strong relationships, and lead a fulfilling life.

Chapter 13: From Surviving to Thriving: How Therapy Can Transform Your Life

Therapy is a powerful tool for personal growth and development. It provides individuals with the opportunity to explore their thoughts, emotions, and behaviors in a safe and supportive environment. Through therapy, individuals can gain insight into themselves, develop coping strategies for life challenges, improve their communication skills, and cultivate self-awareness and self-empowerment. In this article, we will delve into the various benefits of therapy for personal growth and discuss how to overcome the stigma surrounding seeking help. We will also explore how to choose the right therapist, set realistic goals for therapy, build a strong therapeutic relationship, and embrace positive change after therapy.

Understanding the Benefits of Therapy for Personal Growth

Therapy can be incredibly beneficial for personal growth and mental health improvement. It provides individuals with a space to explore their thoughts, emotions, and behaviors in a non-judgmental and supportive environment. Through therapy, individuals can gain insight into themselves and their patterns of thinking and behaving. This self-awareness is crucial for personal growth as it allows individuals to identify areas for improvement and make positive changes in their lives.

There are various types of therapy available, each with its own unique approach and techniques. Cognitive-behavioral therapy (CBT) focuses on identifying and changing negative thought patterns and behaviors. Psychodynamic therapy explores the unconscious mind and past experiences to gain insight into current difficulties. Humanistic therapy emphasizes self-exploration, personal growth, and self-actualization. These are just a few examples of the many types of therapy available.

Identifying When to Seek Professional Help

It can be challenging to determine when it is time to seek professional help through therapy. However, there are several signs that indicate it may be beneficial to reach out to a therapist. These signs include persistent feelings of sadness or hopelessness, difficulty functioning in daily life, excessive worry or anxiety, changes in appetite or sleep patterns, difficulty concentrating, and thoughts of self-harm or suicide. If you are experiencing any of these symptoms, it is important to seek help as soon as possible.

Seeking help early on is crucial for several reasons. First, it allows individuals to address their concerns before they escalate and become more challenging to manage. Early intervention can prevent the development of more severe mental health conditions and improve overall outcomes. Second, therapy can provide individuals with the tools and strategies they need to cope with life challenges effectively. By seeking help early on, individuals can develop healthy coping mechanisms and build resilience.

Overcoming the Stigma of Seeking Therapy

Unfortunately, there is still a significant stigma surrounding therapy and mental health. Many individuals feel ashamed or embarrassed about seeking help, fearing that it makes them weak or flawed. However, seeking therapy is a sign of strength and self-awareness. It takes courage to acknowledge that you need support and to take steps towards improving your mental health.

To overcome the stigma surrounding therapy, it is essential to educate yourself and others about the benefits of seeking help. Talk openly about your experiences with therapy and share how it has positively impacted your life. Surround yourself with supportive individuals who understand the importance of mental health and encourage seeking help when needed. Remember that seeking therapy is a personal decision, and you have the right to prioritize your mental well-being.

Choosing the Right Therapist for Your Needs

Choosing the right therapist is crucial for a successful therapeutic experience. There are several factors to consider when selecting a therapist. First, consider their qualifications and experience. Look for therapists who are licensed and have expertise in the specific area you are seeking help for. For example, if you are struggling with anxiety, look for therapists who specialize in anxiety disorders.

It is also important to consider the therapeutic approach and techniques used by the therapist. Different approaches work better for different individuals, so it is essential to find a therapist whose approach resonates with you. Additionally, consider the therapist's personality and communication style. You should feel comfortable and safe with your therapist, as this will facilitate open and honest communication.

Setting Realistic Goals for Therapy

Setting realistic goals is an important part of the therapeutic process. Goals provide a sense of direction and help measure progress. When setting goals for therapy, it is important to be specific and achievable. Instead of setting a broad goal like "be happier," break it down into smaller, more manageable goals such as "practice self-care activities three times a week" or "challenge negative thoughts with positive affirmations daily."

Setting achievable goals is important because it allows individuals to experience success and build confidence. It is also important to revisit and reassess goals regularly to ensure they are still relevant and meaningful. As individuals progress in therapy, their goals may evolve, and new goals may emerge.

Building Trust and a Strong Therapeutic Relationship

Trust is the foundation of any successful therapeutic relationship. It is essential for individuals to feel safe, heard, and understood by their therapist. Building trust takes time and requires open and honest communication from both parties.

To build trust with your therapist, it is important to be open and transparent about your thoughts, feelings, and experiences. Share your concerns, fears, and goals with your therapist so they can better understand your needs. It is also important to communicate any issues or concerns that arise during therapy openly. A strong therapeutic relationship is built on mutual respect, empathy, and collaboration.

Exploring Your Thoughts and Emotions in Therapy

One of the primary benefits of therapy is the opportunity to explore your thoughts and emotions in a safe and supportive environment. Therapy provides individuals with a space to express themselves freely without fear of judgment or criticism.

Through therapy, individuals can gain insight into their patterns of thinking and behaving. They can explore the underlying causes of their thoughts and emotions and develop a deeper understanding of themselves. This self-exploration is crucial for personal growth as it allows individuals to identify and challenge negative thought patterns and develop healthier ways of thinking.

Developing Coping Strategies for Life Challenges

Life is full of challenges, and therapy can help individuals develop coping strategies to navigate these challenges effectively. Coping strategies are techniques or behaviors that individuals use to manage stress, anxiety, and other difficult emotions.

In therapy, individuals can learn a variety of coping strategies tailored to their specific needs. These strategies may include deep breathing exercises, mindfulness meditation, journaling, physical exercise, and seeking social support. By developing healthy coping mechanisms, individuals can better manage stress and improve their overall well-being.

Learning to Communicate Effectively in Relationships

Effective communication is essential for healthy relationships. Therapy can help individuals improve their communication skills and develop healthier ways of relating to others.

In therapy, individuals can learn active listening skills, assertiveness techniques, and conflict resolution strategies. They can also explore their own communication patterns and identify areas for improvement. By improving their communication skills, individuals can enhance their relationships and foster greater understanding and connection with others.

Cultivating Self-Awareness and Self-Empowerment

Therapy provides individuals with the opportunity to cultivate self-awareness and self-empowerment. Through self-exploration and reflection, individuals can gain a deeper understanding of themselves, their values, and their goals.

Self-awareness is crucial for personal growth as it allows individuals to identify areas for improvement and make positive changes in their lives. It also enables individuals to take responsibility for their thoughts, emotions, and behaviors.

Self-empowerment is the process of gaining control over one's life and making choices that align with one's values and goals. Therapy can help individuals develop the confidence and skills they need to take charge of their lives and create positive change.

Embracing Positive Change and a Thriving Life After Therapy

Therapy is not a quick fix, but rather a journey towards personal growth and self-improvement. It is important to embrace the positive changes that occur during therapy and continue to build upon them after therapy ends.

After therapy, individuals can continue to practice the coping strategies they have learned, maintain open and honest communication in their relationships, and prioritize self-care. It is also important to continue seeking support when needed, whether through therapy or other forms of self-care.

Therapy is a powerful tool for personal growth and development. It provides individuals with the opportunity to explore their thoughts, emotions, and behaviors in a safe and supportive environment. Through therapy, individuals can gain insight into themselves, develop coping strategies for life challenges, improve their communication skills, and cultivate self-awareness and self-empowerment.

If you are experiencing difficulties in your life or struggling with your mental health, do not hesitate to seek professional help through therapy. Remember that seeking help is a sign of strength and self-awareness. By taking steps towards improving your mental well-being, you are investing in your personal growth and overall happiness. Embrace the positive changes that therapy can bring and continue to thrive in your life.

Chapter 14: The Future of Education: Innovations and Trends to Watch Out For

Education is a fundamental pillar of society, shaping the minds and futures of individuals. However, traditional education systems have faced numerous challenges in meeting the diverse needs of learners and preparing them for the rapidly changing world. The need for innovation in education has become more pressing than ever before.

One of the main challenges faced by traditional education systems is the one-size-fits-all approach to learning. In a classroom setting, teachers often have to teach to the average student, leaving behind those who learn at a different pace or have different learning styles. This can lead to disengagement, frustration, and a lack of motivation among students.

Furthermore, the traditional education system often focuses on rote memorization and standardized testing, rather than fostering critical thinking, problem-solving skills, and creativity. This approach does not adequately prepare students for the complex challenges they will face in the real world.

Personalized Learning: The Future of Education

Personalized learning is an innovative approach that tailors education to the individual needs, interests, and abilities of each student. It recognizes that every learner is unique and requires personalized instruction to reach their full potential.

Technology plays a crucial role in enabling personalized learning. Adaptive learning platforms use algorithms to analyze student data and provide personalized recommendations for learning materials and activities. This allows students to learn at their own pace and focus on areas where they need more support.

For example, Khan Academy is a widely recognized personalized learning platform that offers a vast library of educational videos and interactive exercises. Students can progress through the content at their own pace and receive immediate feedback on their performance.

Personalized learning has been shown to improve student engagement, motivation, and academic achievement. It allows students to take ownership of their learning and develop important skills such as self-regulation and self-directed learning.

Artificial Intelligence in Education: The Next Big Thing

Artificial intelligence (AI) has the potential to revolutionize education by providing intelligent tutoring systems, virtual assistants, and automated grading systems. AI can analyze vast amounts of data to identify patterns and personalize instruction for each student.

One example of AI in education is Carnegie Learning's Cognitive Tutor, which uses AI algorithms to provide personalized feedback and guidance to students. The system adapts to each student's learning style and provides targeted interventions to address misconceptions or gaps in knowledge.

AI can also assist teachers in managing administrative tasks, such as grading and lesson planning, allowing them to focus more on individualized instruction and student support.

The benefits of AI in education are numerous. It can provide immediate feedback to students, allowing them to correct mistakes and deepen their understanding. It can also identify areas where students are struggling and provide targeted interventions. Additionally, AI can help bridge the gap between formal and informal learning by providing personalized recommendations for online resources and learning opportunities.

Virtual and Augmented Reality: The Future of Classroom Learning

Virtual reality (VR) and augmented reality (AR) have the potential to transform the classroom experience by creating immersive and interactive learning environments.

VR refers to a computer-generated simulation of a three-dimensional environment that can be explored and interacted with. AR, on the other hand, overlays digital content onto the real world, enhancing the learner's perception of their surroundings.

In education, VR and AR can be used to bring abstract concepts to life, provide virtual field trips, and create simulations for hands-on learning experiences. For example, Google Expeditions is a VR platform that allows students to explore different places around the world without leaving the classroom.

AR can also be used to enhance traditional textbooks by overlaying interactive content such as videos, 3D models, and quizzes. This makes learning more engaging and interactive, helping students retain information better.

The benefits of VR and AR in education are manifold. They can improve student engagement, motivation, and retention of information. They can also provide opportunities for experiential learning and collaboration, as students can interact with virtual objects and work together on projects.

Gamification of Learning: Making Education Fun and Engaging

Gamification is the application of game design principles and mechanics to non-game contexts, such as education. It involves incorporating elements such as points, badges, leaderboards, and challenges into the learning process to make it more fun and engaging.

Gamification has been shown to increase student motivation, engagement, and achievement. It taps into the natural human desire for competition, achievement, and mastery.

For example, Duolingo is a language learning platform that uses gamification to make learning a new language enjoyable. Users earn points for completing lessons, unlock new levels, and compete with friends on leaderboards.

Gamification can also foster collaboration and teamwork by incorporating multiplayer games and group challenges. This promotes social interaction and peer learning, which are important for developing communication and collaboration skills.

Social Learning: The Power of Collaborative Learning

Social learning is an approach that emphasizes learning through social interaction and collaboration. It recognizes that learning is a social process that occurs through observation, imitation, and participation in a community of learners.

In education, social learning can be facilitated through group projects, peer feedback, collaborative problem-solving activities, and online discussion forums.

Social learning has numerous benefits. It promotes active engagement in the learning process, as students are actively involved in discussions and activities. It also helps develop important skills such as communication, teamwork, and critical thinking.

For example, Edmodo is an online platform that allows students to collaborate on projects, share resources, and engage in discussions with their peers. It provides a safe and secure environment for students to connect with each other and learn from one another.

Mobile Learning: The Future of Learning on-the-go

Mobile learning refers to the use of mobile devices such as smartphones and tablets to deliver educational content and provide learning opportunities anytime, anywhere.

Mobile learning has become increasingly popular due to the ubiquity of mobile devices and the flexibility they offer. It allows learners to access educational resources, participate in online courses, and collaborate with peers on the go.

Mobile learning can be particularly beneficial for learners who have limited access to traditional educational resources, such as those in remote areas or developing countries. It can also support lifelong learning by providing opportunities for continuous learning outside of formal education settings.

For example, Coursera is an online learning platform that offers a wide range of courses from top universities and institutions. The platform is accessible through a mobile app, allowing learners to access course materials and complete assignments on their smartphones or tablets.

Mobile learning can enhance the learning experience by providing multimedia content, interactive quizzes, and personalized recommendations based on learner preferences and progress.

Microlearning: Bite-sized Learning for Busy Learners

Microlearning refers to the delivery of small, bite-sized units of learning content that can be consumed in short periods of time. It recognizes that learners today have limited attention spans and busy schedules, and therefore need learning opportunities that are concise and easily digestible.

Microlearning can take various forms, such as short videos, infographics, quizzes, or interactive modules. It allows learners to focus on specific topics or skills and learn at their own pace.

Microlearning has several benefits. It promotes active learning by breaking down complex concepts into smaller, more manageable chunks. It also allows learners to review and reinforce their knowledge quickly and easily.

For example, TED-Ed is an online platform that offers short, animated videos on a wide range of topics. Each video is accompanied by discussion questions and additional resources for further exploration.

Microlearning can be particularly effective for just-in-time learning, where learners need immediate access to specific information or skills. It can also be integrated into larger learning programs as a supplement or reinforcement tool.

Competency-based Learning: Measuring Learning Outcomes

Competency-based learning is an approach that focuses on the mastery of specific skills or competencies rather than the completion of a set curriculum. It emphasizes the demonstration of knowledge and skills through real-world applications and assessments.

In competency-based learning, learners progress at their own pace and move on to the next level of learning only when they have demonstrated mastery of the current level. This allows learners to focus on areas where they need more support and spend less time on topics they have already mastered.

Competency-based learning can be facilitated through project-based assessments, portfolios, simulations, and performance tasks. It provides a more authentic and meaningful way of measuring learning outcomes compared to traditional standardized tests.

For example, Western Governors University is an online university that offers competency-based degree programs. Students are assessed based on their ability to demonstrate specific competencies through a series of assessments and projects.

Competency-based learning promotes student agency and self-directed learning. It also prepares learners for the real world by focusing on the development of practical skills and abilities.

Data-driven Learning: The Future of Assessment and Evaluation

Data-driven learning refers to the use of data analytics and insights to inform instructional decisions and improve learning outcomes. It involves collecting, analyzing, and interpreting data on student performance, engagement, and progress to identify areas for improvement and personalize instruction.

Data-driven learning can be facilitated through learning analytics platforms that track student interactions with digital learning materials, online assessments, and other educational resources. These platforms provide real-time feedback to teachers and students, allowing them to make informed decisions about instruction and support.

Data-driven learning has several benefits. It allows teachers to identify struggling students early on and provide targeted interventions. It also helps identify effective teaching strategies and resources that can be shared with other educators.

For example, ALEKS is an adaptive learning platform that uses data analytics to provide personalized instruction and assessment in math. The platform tracks student progress and provides real-time feedback to both students and teachers.

Data-driven learning can also support formative assessment, where students receive ongoing feedback and have the opportunity to reflect on their learning and make improvements.

The Future of Education is Here

In conclusion, the need for innovation in education has become more pressing than ever before. Traditional education systems face numerous challenges in meeting the diverse needs of learners and preparing them for the rapidly changing world.

Personalized learning, artificial intelligence, virtual and augmented reality, gamification, social learning, mobile learning, microlearning, competency-based learning, data-driven learning are all innovative approaches that have the potential to transform education for the better.

These approaches recognize that every learner is unique and requires personalized instruction to reach their full potential. They leverage technology to provide individualized instruction, create immersive and interactive learning environments, make learning fun and engaging, promote collaboration and teamwork, provide learning opportunities on-the-go, deliver bite-sized learning opportunities for busy learners, measure learning outcomes through competency-based assessments, and inform instructional decisions through data analytics.

The future of education is here, and it is exciting. By embracing innovation and leveraging technology, we can create a more inclusive, engaging, and effective education system that prepares learners for success in the 21st century.

Chapter 15: Advocacy in the Digital Age: Leveraging Technology for Social Impact

Advocacy is the act of supporting a cause or promoting a particular viewpoint in order to bring about social change. It involves raising awareness, influencing public opinion, and mobilizing support for a specific issue or cause. Advocacy plays a crucial role in promoting social change by giving a voice to marginalized communities, challenging unjust policies, and pushing for systemic reforms.

Advocacy is important because it helps to address social injustices and inequalities. It gives a platform to those who are often unheard and marginalized, allowing them to share their experiences and perspectives. Through advocacy, individuals and organizations can work together to challenge discriminatory practices, advocate for policy changes, and create a more inclusive society.

The Impact of Technology on Advocacy: An Overview

Technology has revolutionized the way advocacy is conducted and has significantly expanded its reach and impact. With the advent of the internet and digital technologies, advocacy efforts can now reach a global audience in real-time. Technology has made it easier for advocates to connect with like-minded individuals, share information, and mobilize support for their cause.

One of the key ways technology has changed the landscape of advocacy is through the use of social media platforms. Social media allows advocates to reach a wide audience, engage with supporters, and amplify their message. It provides a platform for sharing stories, raising awareness, and organizing campaigns. Additionally, technology has also enabled the use of crowdfunding platforms, big data analysis, online petitions, virtual reality, and artificial intelligence in advocacy efforts.

Social Media: A Powerful Tool for Advocacy

Social media has revolutionized advocacy by providing a powerful platform for individuals and organizations to raise awareness about social issues and mobilize support. Platforms like Facebook, Twitter, Instagram, and YouTube have become essential tools for advocates to share their message, engage with supporters, and create online communities.

Social media allows advocates to reach a global audience instantly and at a low cost. It enables them to share stories, images, and videos that can evoke emotions and inspire action. Social media also facilitates two-way communication, allowing advocates to engage with their audience, respond to questions and concerns, and build relationships with supporters.

There have been numerous successful social media advocacy campaigns that have brought about significant social change. For example, the #MeToo movement gained momentum through social media, with survivors of sexual harassment and assault sharing their stories and raising awareness about the prevalence of such issues. The Black Lives Matter movement also gained traction through social media, with activists using hashtags and viral videos to draw attention to police brutality and systemic racism.

Crowdfunding: The Power of the Crowd

Crowdfunding is a method of raising funds for a project or cause by collecting small contributions from a large number of people, typically via online platforms. Crowdfunding has become an increasingly popular tool for advocacy, as it allows individuals and organizations to raise money for their cause directly from the public.

Crowdfunding has been used in advocacy to fundraise for various initiatives, such as disaster relief efforts, medical treatments, environmental conservation projects, and social justice campaigns. It provides an alternative funding source for advocates who may not have access to traditional sources of funding.

One notable example of a successful crowdfunding campaign is the ALS Ice Bucket Challenge. In 2014, the ALS Association launched a campaign where participants would pour a bucket of ice water over their heads and challenge others to do the same or donate to ALS research. The campaign went viral on social media, resulting in millions of dollars in donations and increased awareness about ALS.

Big Data: Harnessing Information for Social Impact

Big data refers to large sets of data that can be analyzed to reveal patterns, trends, and associations. In advocacy, big data analysis can be used to gather insights about social issues, identify areas for intervention, and measure the impact of advocacy efforts.

Big data has been used in advocacy to inform policy decisions, target resources effectively, and monitor progress towards social change goals. For example, organizations working on poverty alleviation can use big data analysis to identify areas with the highest poverty rates, understand the underlying causes, and develop targeted interventions.

One successful example of big data advocacy is the DataKind project. DataKind is a nonprofit organization that connects data scientists with social change organizations to help them leverage data for impact. Through their projects, DataKind has helped organizations use big data analysis to address issues such as human trafficking, education inequality, and disaster response.

Online Petitions: Mobilizing Support for a Cause

Online petitions have become a popular tool for advocacy, allowing individuals to express their support or opposition to a particular issue or cause. Online petition platforms enable advocates to collect signatures from people who share their concerns and mobilize support for their cause.

Online petitions are effective because they provide a simple and accessible way for individuals to take action and make their voices heard. They can be easily shared on social media platforms, allowing advocates to reach a wider audience and gather more signatures.

There have been numerous successful online petition campaigns that have brought about significant change. For example, the Change.org petition calling for justice for Trayvon Martin, an unarmed African American teenager who was shot and killed by a neighborhood watch volunteer, garnered millions of signatures and helped to spark a national conversation about racial profiling and gun violence.

Virtual Reality: Creating Empathy and Understanding

Virtual reality (VR) technology has been used in advocacy to create immersive experiences that can evoke empathy and understanding. VR allows users to step into someone else's shoes and experience a situation firsthand, which can be a powerful tool for raising awareness about social issues.

VR has been used in advocacy to shed light on issues such as refugee experiences, environmental degradation, and human rights violations. By immersing users in these experiences, VR can help to bridge the empathy gap and inspire action.

One successful example of VR advocacy is the United Nations' "Clouds Over Sidra" project. The project used VR to transport viewers to a Syrian refugee camp, allowing them to see the daily lives of refugees and gain a deeper understanding of their experiences. The project was highly effective in raising awareness about the refugee crisis and generating support for humanitarian efforts.

Artificial Intelligence: Enhancing Advocacy Efforts

Artificial intelligence (AI) has the potential to enhance advocacy efforts by automating tasks, analyzing data, and providing personalized recommendations. AI can help advocates to streamline their operations, target their messaging effectively, and make evidence-based decisions.

AI has been used in advocacy to analyze large amounts of data, identify patterns and trends, and generate insights. For example, AI algorithms can analyze social media data to understand public sentiment towards a particular issue or identify key influencers who can help amplify a message.

One successful example of AI advocacy is the Project Debater developed by IBM. Project Debater is an AI system that can engage in debates with humans on complex topics. The system uses natural language processing and machine learning algorithms to analyze arguments, generate counterarguments, and provide evidence-based responses. Project Debater has been used in debates on topics such as universal basic income and space exploration, helping to inform public discourse and shape policy decisions.

The Importance of Digital Literacy in Advocacy

Digital literacy is the ability to use digital technologies effectively and responsibly. In advocacy, digital literacy is crucial because it enables advocates to navigate online platforms, create compelling content, engage with supporters, and protect their privacy and security.

Digital literacy is important for advocacy because it allows advocates to leverage technology effectively to promote their cause. It enables them to use social media platforms, crowdfunding platforms, big data analysis tools, online petition platforms, virtual reality technologies, and artificial intelligence systems to advance their goals.

To improve digital literacy for advocacy, individuals and organizations can participate in training programs, workshops, and online courses that focus on digital skills. They can also seek mentorship from experienced advocates who have successfully used technology in their advocacy efforts.

Challenges and Limitations of Technology in Advocacy

While technology has greatly enhanced advocacy efforts, it also presents challenges and limitations that advocates need to be aware of and address. Some of the challenges include:

1. Access: Not everyone has equal access to technology and the internet, which can create a digital divide and limit the reach of advocacy efforts. Advocates need to ensure that their message reaches all segments of society, including those who may not have access to technology.

2. Privacy and Security: The use of technology in advocacy raises concerns about privacy and security. Advocates need to be mindful of the data they collect, how it is stored and used, and take steps to protect the privacy and security of their supporters.

3. Misinformation and Disinformation: The spread of misinformation and disinformation on social media platforms can undermine advocacy efforts. Advocates need to be vigilant in verifying information before sharing it and educate their audience about how to identify reliable sources of information.

4. Overreliance on Technology: While technology can enhance advocacy efforts, it should not replace human connection and grassroots organizing. Advocates need to strike a balance between using technology effectively and maintaining personal relationships with supporters.

To overcome these challenges, advocates can collaborate with organizations that focus on bridging the digital divide, prioritize privacy and security in their technology use, promote media literacy among their audience, and combine online advocacy with offline organizing.

The Future of Advocacy in the Digital Age

The potential of technology in advocacy is vast, and its impact will continue to grow in the future. As new technologies emerge, advocates need to adapt and embrace these tools to enhance their efforts and promote social change.

The future of advocacy in the digital age will likely involve the integration of various technologies, such as artificial intelligence, virtual reality, and big data analysis. Advocates will need to continue to prioritize digital literacy, adapt to new platforms and tools, and find innovative ways to engage with their audience.

By harnessing the power of technology, advocates can amplify their message, mobilize support, and bring about meaningful social change. However, it is important to remember that technology is just a tool - it is the passion, dedication, and commitment of advocates that ultimately drive social change.

Chapter 16: From First Dates to Forever: Tips for Making Your Relationship Last

Maintaining a healthy relationship is crucial for our overall well-being and happiness. Whether it's a romantic partnership, a friendship, or a family bond, healthy relationships provide us with support, love, and a sense of belonging. However, maintaining a healthy relationship requires effort and dedication from both parties involved. In this article, we will explore various aspects of maintaining a healthy relationship and provide tips and strategies for improving communication, keeping the romance alive, resolving conflicts, building trust and honesty, spending quality time together, supporting each other, embracing differences, managing expectations, setting goals as a couple, trying new things, recognizing warning signs, and seeking help when needed.

Communication is Key: How to Talk to Your Partner

Effective communication is the foundation of any healthy relationship. It allows us to express our needs, desires, and concerns while also listening to our partner's perspective. Good communication helps build trust and understanding between partners and prevents misunderstandings and conflicts from escalating.

To improve communication with your partner, it's important to practice active listening. This means giving your full attention to your partner when they are speaking and avoiding distractions such as phones or television. Show empathy by trying to understand their point of view and validate their feelings. Avoid interrupting or jumping to conclusions before they have finished speaking.

Another important aspect of communication is expressing yourself clearly and assertively. Use "I" statements to express your thoughts and feelings instead of blaming or criticizing your partner. Be specific about what you want or need from them and avoid making assumptions about their intentions or motivations.

Keeping the Spark Alive: Ways to Keep the Romance Going

Romance is an essential component of a healthy relationship. It keeps the passion alive and strengthens the emotional connection between partners. However, as time goes on, it's easy for the romance to fade away amidst the demands of daily life.

To keep the romance alive, it's important to prioritize quality time together. Plan regular date nights or weekend getaways where you can focus on each other without distractions. Surprise your partner with small gestures of love and affection, such as leaving them a sweet note or preparing their favorite meal.

Get creative with your romantic gestures. Plan a picnic in the park, take a dance class together, or write each other love letters. The key is to make an effort to keep the romance alive and show your partner that they are still the most important person in your life.

Fighting Fair: Tips for Resolving Conflict in a Healthy Way

Conflict is inevitable in any relationship, but it's how we handle it that determines the health of our relationship. When conflicts arise, it's important to approach them with a mindset of finding a solution rather than winning an argument.

One of the most important tips for resolving conflict in a healthy way is to practice active listening. This means giving your full attention to your partner and trying to understand their perspective without interrupting or becoming defensive. Avoid personal attacks or criticism and focus on the issue at hand.

It's also important to take responsibility for your own actions and emotions. Instead of blaming your partner, express how their behavior made you feel and what you need from them moving forward. Use "I" statements instead of "you" statements to avoid sounding accusatory.

Finding common ground and compromising is crucial for resolving conflicts. Look for areas where you can meet halfway and find solutions that work for both of you. Remember that it's okay to take a break if emotions are running high and revisit the conversation when you both feel calmer.

Trust and Honesty: Building a Strong Foundation for Your Relationship

Trust and honesty are the pillars of a healthy relationship. Without trust, there can be no true intimacy or emotional connection between partners. Building trust takes time and effort, but it's essential for the long-term success of any relationship.

To build trust, it's important to be honest and transparent with your partner. Avoid keeping secrets or withholding information that could be important to the relationship. Be reliable and follow through on your commitments. Trust is built through consistent actions over time.

It's also important to trust your partner and give them the benefit of the doubt. Avoid jumping to conclusions or assuming the worst about their intentions. Trust requires vulnerability and a willingness to let go of control.

If trust has been broken in the relationship, it's important to address it openly and honestly. Seek professional help if needed to work through the issues and rebuild trust. Remember that trust takes time to rebuild, and it's okay to set boundaries and take things slow.

Quality Time: The Importance of Spending Time

Together

In our busy lives, it's easy to prioritize work, chores, and other responsibilities over spending quality time with our partners. However, quality time is essential for maintaining a healthy relationship. It allows us to connect on a deeper level, strengthen our emotional bond, and create lasting memories together.

Make it a priority to spend dedicated time together each day, even if it's just for a few minutes. Put away distractions such as phones or television and focus on each other. Ask about each other's day, share your thoughts and feelings, and truly listen to what your partner has to say.

Plan regular date nights or weekend getaways where you can focus solely on each other without distractions. Try new activities together or revisit old hobbies that you used to enjoy as a couple. The key is to make an effort to spend quality time together and show your partner that they are a priority in your life.

Supporting Each Other: How to Be a Good Partner

Supporting your partner is an essential aspect of a healthy relationship. It means being there for them during both the good times and the bad, offering encouragement and understanding, and helping them achieve their goals and dreams.

To be a good partner, it's important to practice active listening and show empathy. Validate your partner's feelings and offer support without judgment. Be their cheerleader and celebrate their successes, no matter how big or small.

Offer practical support by helping out with household chores, running errands, or taking care of the kids. Show interest in their hobbies and passions and encourage them to pursue their dreams. Be a source of emotional support by being there for them during difficult times and offering a shoulder to lean on.

Remember that supporting your partner is a two-way street. It's important to communicate your needs and desires to your partner and ask for their support when needed. A healthy relationship is built on mutual support and understanding.

Embracing Differences: Celebrating What Makes Your Relationship Unique

Every relationship is unique, and it's important to embrace and celebrate the differences that make your relationship special. Our differences can complement each other and bring new perspectives and experiences into the relationship.

Instead of trying to change or control your partner, embrace their individuality and appreciate what makes them unique. Celebrate their strengths and talents, even if they are different from your own. Remember that diversity can enrich our lives and bring new opportunities for growth and learning.

It's also important to communicate openly about your differences and find ways to compromise when conflicts arise. Respect each other's boundaries and find common ground where you can both feel comfortable and supported.

Managing Expectations: How to Avoid Disappointment and Frustration

Unrealistic expectations can lead to disappointment and frustration in a relationship. It's important trant to have open and honest conversations about your expectations for the relationship, both individually and as a couple.

Communicate your needs and desires to your partner, but also be willing to listen to their perspective. Find common ground where you can both feel satisfied and supported. Remember that compromise is essential in any relationship and that it's okay to adjust your expectations as the relationship evolves.

Avoid comparing your relationship to others or to unrealistic standards portrayed in the media. Every relationship is unique, and what works for others may not work for you. Focus on your own relationship and what makes it special.

Growing Together: Setting Goals and Working Towards Them as a Couple

Setting goals as a couple is an important aspect of maintaining a healthy relationship. It allows you to create a shared vision for the future and work towards common objectives. Setting goals together can strengthen your bond and provide a sense of purpose and direction.

Start by discussing your individual goals and dreams with your partner. Identify areas where your goals align and find ways to support each other in achieving them. Set both short-term and long-term goals that are realistic and achievable.

Break down your goals into smaller, manageable steps and create a plan for achieving them. Celebrate each milestone along the way and adjust your plan as needed. Remember that setbacks are a normal part of the process, and it's important to support each other during difficult times.

Keeping Things Fresh: Trying New Things and Keeping the Relationship Exciting

Trying new things is essential for keeping the relationship exciting and preventing it from becoming stagnant. It allows you to create new memories together, learn new skills, and explore new interests.

Make it a priority to try something new as a couple on a regular basis. This could be trying a new restaurant, taking a dance class, going on a weekend getaway, or exploring a new hobby together. The key is to step out of your comfort zone and embrace new experiences together.

Keep the element of surprise alive by planning surprises for each other. This could be surprising your partner with tickets to their favorite concert or planning a spontaneous weekend trip. The element of surprise keeps the relationship exciting and shows your partner that you are thinking of them.

Recognizing Warning Signs: Knowing When to Seek Help for Your Relationship

It's important to recognize the warning signs of a troubled relationship and seek help when needed. Ignoring or dismissing these signs can lead to further damage and unhappiness in the relationship.

Some common warning signs of a troubled relationship include constant arguing, lack of trust or respect, emotional or physical abuse, lack of intimacy or connection, and feeling unhappy or unfulfilled in the relationship.

If you notice any of these warning signs, it's important to address them openly and honestly with your partner. Seek professional help if needed, such as couples therapy or counseling. Remember that seeking help is a sign of strength and a willingness to work on the relationship.

Maintaining a healthy relationship requires effort and dedication from both partners involved. It's important to prioritize effective communication, keep the romance alive, resolve conflicts in a healthy way, build trust and honesty, spend quality time together, support each other, embrace differences, manage expectations, set goals as a couple, try new things, recognize warning signs, and seek help when needed.

By following these tips and strategies, you can create a strong foundation for your relationship and ensure its long-term success.

Remember that relationships require ongoing work and commitment, but the rewards are well worth it.

Chapter 17: The Art of Standing Alone: Celebrating Independence Day

Independence Day is a significant holiday that celebrates the freedom and independence of a nation. It is a time to reflect on the importance of standing alone, embracing solitude, honoring our individuality, and pursuing our passions. This article will explore the power of independence and self-reliance, the beauty of solitude and self-expression, the strength of resilience and self-discovery, the importance of self-care and pursuing our passions, and the power of building strong relationships on our own terms. Independence Day is not only a time to celebrate the freedom of a nation, but also an opportunity to reflect, recharge, and renew our commitment to ourselves.

The Power of Independence: Why Standing Alone Matters

Independence is a powerful concept that holds great significance in our lives. It is the ability to stand alone, make decisions for ourselves, and take responsibility for our actions. Being independent allows us to have control over our own lives and make choices that align with our values and goals. It gives us the freedom to pursue our passions, express ourselves authentically, and live life on our own terms.

There are numerous benefits to standing alone and being independent. It fosters self-confidence and self-reliance, as we learn to trust ourselves and our abilities. It encourages personal growth and development, as we are forced to overcome challenges and make decisions without relying on others. Independence also promotes resilience and adaptability, as we learn to navigate through life's ups and downs with grace and strength.

There are many examples of successful independent individuals who have made significant contributions to society. Entrepreneurs like Steve Jobs and Elon Musk have revolutionized industries through their innovative ideas and unwavering determination. Artists like Frida Kahlo and Vincent van Gogh have created timeless works of art that continue to inspire generations. These individuals have shown us that standing alone can lead to great achievements and leave a lasting impact on the world.

The Art of Self-Reliance: Celebrating Independence Day

Independence Day is a time to celebrate self-reliance and the ability to take care of ourselves. It is a day to reflect on our own strengths and capabilities, and to appreciate the freedom that comes with being self-reliant. On this day, we can cultivate self-reliance by engaging in activities that promote independence, such as setting goals and working towards them, learning new skills, and taking responsibility for our own well-being.

There are many ways to cultivate self-reliance in our daily lives. We can start by setting realistic goals and breaking them down into smaller, manageable tasks. By achieving these goals on our own, we build confidence in our abilities and develop a sense of self-reliance. We can also learn new skills and expand our knowledge base, whether it's through taking classes, reading books, or seeking out new experiences. By continuously learning and growing, we become more self-reliant and adaptable in different situations.

Being self-reliant has numerous benefits for our overall well-being. It allows us to have a sense of control over our lives and make decisions that align with our values and goals. It fosters independence and resilience, as we learn to navigate through challenges and setbacks on our own. Being self-reliant also promotes personal growth and development, as we take ownership of our actions and strive to become the best version of ourselves.

Embracing Solitude: Finding Joy in Being Alone

Solitude is often seen as a negative concept in today's society, but it is actually an important aspect of our well-being. Embracing solitude allows us to disconnect from the outside world and connect with ourselves on a deeper level. It gives us the opportunity to reflect, recharge, and gain clarity about our thoughts, feelings, and desires.

There are many ways to enjoy being alone and embrace solitude. We can start by carving out dedicated time for ourselves each day, whether it's through meditation, journaling, or engaging in a hobby that brings us joy. By creating space for solitude, we can recharge our energy and gain a sense of inner peace. We can also use this time to reflect on our goals, values, and priorities, and make any necessary adjustments to align our lives with what truly matters to us.

Embracing solitude has numerous benefits for our mental and emotional well-being. It allows us to recharge and rejuvenate, reducing stress and promoting overall happiness. Solitude also fosters self-awareness and self-discovery, as we have the opportunity to explore our inner worlds without distractions. By embracing solitude, we can cultivate a deeper sense of self-acceptance and self-love, leading to greater fulfillment and contentment in our lives.

The Freedom of Self-Expression: Honoring Our Individuality

Self-expression is a fundamental aspect of our humanity. It is the ability to communicate our thoughts, feelings, and ideas in a way that is authentic and true to ourselves. Honoring our individuality means embracing our unique qualities and expressing them freely without fear of judgment or rejection.

Self-expression can take many forms, from art and music to writing and speaking. It is about finding ways to communicate who we are and what we believe in, whether it's through creative outlets or simply sharing our thoughts and opinions with others. By expressing ourselves authentically, we not only honor our individuality but also inspire others to do the same.

There are many benefits to honoring our individuality and embracing self-expression. It allows us to connect with others on a deeper level, as we share our true selves with the world. Self-expression also promotes personal growth and self-acceptance, as we learn to embrace all aspects of who we are. By honoring our individuality, we can live a life that is true to ourselves and find fulfillment and happiness in the process.

Celebrating the Courage to Be Different: Independence Day Reflections

Being different is often seen as a negative thing in society, but it is actually a strength. Embracing our uniqueness and celebrating our differences allows us to stand out from the crowd and make a positive impact in the world. Independence Day is a time to reflect on the courage it takes to be different and honor those who have embraced their uniqueness.

There are many examples of individuals who have embraced their uniqueness and made significant contributions to society. People like Malala Yousafzai, who fought for girls' education in Pakistan despite facing threats and violence, and Rosa Parks, who refused to give up her seat on a bus during the civil rights movement, have shown us the power of embracing our differences and standing up for what we believe in. These individuals have not only made a difference in their own lives but have also inspired others to do the same.

Embracing our differences has numerous benefits for our personal growth and well-being. It allows us to live authentically and align our lives with our values and beliefs. Being different also fosters creativity and innovation, as we bring unique perspectives and ideas to the table. By celebrating the courage to be different, we can create a world that values diversity and embraces individuality.

The Beauty of Self-Discovery: Exploring Our Inner Worlds

Self-discovery is an ongoing journey of exploring our inner worlds and uncovering our true selves. It is about gaining a deeper understanding of who we are, what we want, and what brings us joy and fulfillment. Independence Day is a time to reflect on the importance of self-discovery and embrace the beauty of exploring our inner worlds.

There are many ways to explore our inner worlds and embark on a journey of self-discovery. We can start by practicing self-reflection and introspection, whether it's through journaling, meditation, or engaging in activities that bring us joy and allow us to connect with ourselves on a deeper level. By taking the time to listen to our inner voice and pay attention to our thoughts and feelings, we can gain valuable insights about ourselves and what truly matters to us.

Self-discovery has numerous benefits for our personal growth and well-being. It allows us to gain a deeper understanding of ourselves and our desires, leading to greater clarity and purpose in our lives. Self-discovery also promotes self-acceptance and self-love, as we learn to embrace all aspects of who we are. By exploring our inner worlds, we can cultivate a sense of inner peace and fulfillment that extends into all areas of our lives.

The Strength of Resilience: Overcoming Challenges on Our Own

Resilience is the ability to bounce back from adversity and overcome challenges with strength and grace. It is an important quality to cultivate in our lives, as it allows us to navigate through life's ups and downs with resilience and determination. Independence Day is a time to reflect on the importance of resilience and celebrate the strength it takes to overcome challenges on our own.

There are many ways to build resilience in our lives. We can start by reframing challenges as opportunities for growth and learning, rather than obstacles that hold us back. By shifting our mindset and embracing a positive outlook, we can approach challenges with resilience and determination. We can also practice self-care and prioritize our well-being, as taking care of ourselves physically, mentally, and emotionally allows us to build the strength and resilience needed to overcome challenges.

Building resilience has numerous benefits for our overall well-being. It allows us to navigate through life's challenges with grace and strength, reducing stress and promoting mental and emotional well-being. Resilience also fosters personal growth and development, as we learn from our experiences and become stronger and more adaptable in the process. By celebrating the strength of resilience, we can overcome challenges and create a life that is filled with joy, fulfillment, and success.

The Importance of Self-Care: Nurturing Our Minds, Bodies, and Souls

Self-care is an essential aspect of our well-being. It is the practice of nurturing our minds, bodies, and souls to ensure that we are taking care of ourselves holistically. Independence Day is a time to reflect on the importance of self-care and prioritize our well-being.

There are many ways to practice self-care in our daily lives. We can start by prioritizing our physical health through regular exercise, nutritious eating, and adequate sleep. Taking care of our bodies allows us to have the energy and vitality needed to pursue our passions and live life to the fullest. We can also prioritize our mental and emotional well-being by engaging in activities that bring us joy and reduce stress, such as practicing mindfulness, spending time in nature, or engaging in creative outlets.

Practicing self-care has numerous benefits for our overall well-being. It allows us to recharge and rejuvenate, reducing stress and promoting mental and emotional well-being. Self-care also fosters self-love and self-acceptance, as we prioritize our own needs and make ourselves a priority. By practicing self-care, we can create a life that is filled with joy, balance, and fulfillment.

The Gift of Time: Using Our Independence to Pursue Our Passions

Time is a precious gift that we have the freedom to use as we please. Independence Day is a time to reflect on the importance of using our independence to pursue our passions and live a life that is aligned with our values and desires.

There are many ways to use our independence to pursue our passions. We can start by identifying what brings us joy and fulfillment, whether it's a hobby, a career, or a cause that we are passionate about. By aligning our lives with our passions, we can create a sense of purpose and fulfillment that extends into all areas of our lives. We can also prioritize our time and energy towards our passions, setting aside dedicated time each day or week to engage in activities that bring us joy and allow us to pursue our passions.

Using our independence to pursue our passions has numerous benefits for our overall well-being. It allows us to live a life that is true to ourselves and aligned with our values and desires. Pursuing our passions also promotes personal growth and self-fulfillment, as we engage in activities that bring us joy and allow us to express ourselves authentically. By using our independence to pursue our passions, we can create a life that is filled with purpose, joy, and fulfillment.

The Power of Connection: Building Strong Relationships on Our Own Terms

Building strong relationships is an important aspect of our lives. It allows us to connect with others on a deeper level and create meaningful connections that bring joy and fulfillment. Independence Day is a time to reflect on the power of connection and celebrate the ability to build strong relationships on our own terms.

There are many ways to build strong relationships on our own terms. We can start by setting boundaries and communicating our needs and expectations in relationships. By being clear about what we want and need from others, we can create relationships that are based on mutual respect and understanding. We can also surround ourselves with people who support and uplift us, whether it's friends, family, or mentors who inspire us to be the best version of ourselves.

Building strong relationships has numerous benefits for our overall well-being. It allows us to feel supported and loved, reducing feelings of loneliness and promoting mental and emotional well-being. Strong relationships also foster personal growth and development, as we learn from others and gain new perspectives on life. By building strong relationships on our own terms, we can create a support system that uplifts and empowers us to live a life that is true to ourselves.

Celebrating Independence Day: A Time to Reflect, Recharge, and Renew Our Commitment to Ourselves

Independence Day is not only a time to celebrate the freedom of a nation but also an opportunity to reflect, recharge, and renew our commitment to ourselves. It is a time to honor our independence and prioritize our well-being.

There are many ways to reflect, recharge, and renew our commitment to ourselves on Independence Day. We can start by taking the time to reflect on our goals, values, and priorities, and make any necessary adjustments to align our lives with what truly matters to us. We can also recharge our energy by engaging in activities that bring us joy and allow us to connect with ourselves on a deeper level. By prioritizing our well-being and making ourselves a priority, we can renew our commitment to living a life that is true to ourselves.

Reflecting, recharging, and renewing our commitment to ourselves has numerous benefits for our overall well-being. It allows us to gain clarity and purpose in our lives, reducing stress and promoting mental and emotional well-being. Reflecting, recharging, and renewing our commitment to ourselves also fosters self-love and self-acceptance, as we prioritize our own needs and make ourselves a priority. By celebrating Independence Day as a time of reflection, recharge, and renewal, we can create a life that is more balanced and fulfilling. Taking the time to reflect on our goals, values, and priorities helps us make necessary adjustments and realign ourselves with what truly matters to us. This process of self-reflection allows us to identify areas of growth and improvement, leading to personal development and increased self-awareness. Additionally, recharging our energy and taking care of our physical, mental, and emotional well-being is crucial for maintaining a healthy lifestyle. By engaging in activities that bring us joy and relaxation, we can reduce stress levels and improve our overall quality of life. Finally, renewing our commitment to ourselves means honoring our own needs and desires, setting boundaries, and making choices that align with our values. This practice of self-care and self-love not only benefits us individually but also strengthens our relationships with others as we show up as our best selves. Overall, celebrating Independence Day as a time of reflection, recharge, and renewal allows us to create a life that is more intentional, balanced, and aligned with our true selves.

Chapter 18: Surviving and Thriving: 17 Coping Strategies for Overcoming Adversity

Adversity is a part of life that we all face at some point. It refers to the challenges, difficulties, and setbacks that we encounter along our journey. Adversity can come in many forms, such as the loss of a loved one, financial struggles, health issues, or relationship problems. It is a natural and inevitable part of the human experience.

The impact of adversity on our mental and physical health cannot be underestimated. It can lead to stress, anxiety, depression, and other mental health issues. It can also take a toll on our physical well-being, leading to sleep problems, weakened immune system, and chronic health conditions. Adversity can be overwhelming and can make us feel helpless and hopeless.

Coping strategies are essential tools that can help us navigate through adversity and overcome its challenges. They are the skills and techniques that we use to manage stress, regulate our emotions, and maintain our well-being. Coping strategies are not about avoiding or denying the difficulties we face but rather about finding healthy ways to deal with them.

Coping Strategy #1: Accepting the Situation and Your Emotions

One of the most important coping strategies when facing adversity is accepting the situation and your emotions. Acceptance involves acknowledging the reality of the situation and coming to terms with it. It means letting go of resistance and allowing yourself to feel whatever emotions arise.

Accepting the situation can be challenging because it requires us to confront painful truths and let go of our expectations. However, it is an essential step towards healing and moving forward. When we accept the situation, we free ourselves from the burden of resistance and open ourselves up to new possibilities.

Accepting your emotions is also crucial in coping with adversity. It is normal to experience a wide range of emotions when facing difficult times, such as sadness, anger, fear, or frustration. Instead of suppressing or avoiding these emotions, it is important to allow yourself to feel them fully. Emotions are a natural response to adversity, and by accepting them, you can process and release them in a healthy way.

Mindfulness plays a significant role in acceptance. Mindfulness is the practice of being fully present in the moment and non-judgmentally aware of your thoughts, feelings, and sensations. By cultivating mindfulness, you can observe your emotions without getting caught up in them. This allows you to create space for acceptance and develop a more compassionate and understanding relationship with yourself.

Coping Strategy #2: Building a Support System

Building a support system is another crucial coping strategy when facing adversity. Social support plays a significant role in our well-being and resilience. Having people who understand, listen, and support us can make a world of difference in how we navigate through difficult times.

The importance of social support cannot be overstated. It provides us with emotional validation, practical assistance, and a sense of belonging. It helps us feel less alone and more understood. Research has shown that individuals with strong social support networks have better mental health outcomes and are more resilient in the face of adversity.

Building a support system starts with identifying the people in your life who are supportive and trustworthy. These can be family members, friends, colleagues, or even support groups. Reach out to them and let them know what you are going through. Be open and honest about your needs and ask for their help and support.

Different types of support are available depending on your needs. Emotional support involves having someone to talk to, vent your feelings, and receive empathy and understanding. Practical support involves receiving assistance with daily tasks or practical advice on how to navigate through challenges. Informational support involves getting information or resources that can help you better understand and cope with your situation.

Coping Strategy #3: Practicing Self-Care and Mindfulness

Practicing self-care and mindfulness is another essential coping strategy when facing adversity. Self-care involves taking care of your physical, emotional, and mental well-being. It is about prioritizing your needs and engaging in activities that nourish and rejuvenate you.

Self-care is not selfish; it is necessary for your overall well-being. When you take care of yourself, you are better equipped to handle the challenges that come your way. It helps you recharge, reduce stress, and maintain a positive mindset.

There are many ways to practice self-care and mindfulness. Physical self-care involves engaging in activities that promote physical health, such as exercise, healthy eating, and getting enough sleep. Emotional self-care involves engaging in activities that nurture your emotions, such as journaling, practicing gratitude, or engaging in hobbies you enjoy.

Mindfulness is a powerful practice that can help you stay present and grounded in the midst of adversity. It involves paying attention to the present moment without judgment. Mindfulness can be practiced through meditation, deep breathing exercises, or simply by bringing your attention to the sensations in your body.

Coping Strategy #4: Finding Meaning and Purpose in Life

Finding meaning and purpose in life is another important coping strategy when facing adversity. It involves discovering what truly matters to you and aligning your actions with your values and passions. When you have a sense of purpose, it gives you a reason to keep going even in the face of challenges.

Finding meaning and purpose can be a transformative process. It requires self-reflection and exploration of your values, interests, and goals. It involves asking yourself what brings you joy, what makes you feel fulfilled, and what legacy you want to leave behind.

There are different ways to find meaning and purpose in life. One way is through connecting with others and making a positive impact on their lives. This can be through volunteering, mentoring, or engaging in acts of kindness. Another way is through pursuing your passions and interests. This can be through engaging in creative activities, learning new skills, or pursuing a career that aligns with your values.

Finding meaning and purpose is not a one-time event; it is an ongoing process. It requires continuous self-reflection and adjustment as you grow and evolve. By finding meaning and purpose, you can find a sense of direction and motivation to overcome adversity and thrive in life.

Coping Strategy #5: Focusing on the Present Moment

Focusing on the present moment is another powerful coping strategy when facing adversity. It involves bringing your attention to the here and now and letting go of worries about the past or future. When you focus on the present moment, you can find peace, clarity, and a sense of control.

The benefits of focusing on the present moment are numerous. It helps reduce stress, anxiety, and overwhelm. It allows you to fully engage in the tasks at hand and make better decisions. It also helps you appreciate the small joys and beauty in life that may otherwise go unnoticed.

Practicing mindfulness is a powerful way to focus on the present moment. Mindfulness involves paying attention to your thoughts, feelings, and sensations without judgment. It can be practiced through meditation, mindful eating, or simply by bringing your attention to your breath or the sensations in your body.

There are different techniques and practices available to help you stay present. One technique is grounding, which involves using your senses to bring yourself back to the present moment. This can be done by focusing on the sensations in your body or noticing the details of your surroundings.

Another practice is gratitude, which involves focusing on what you are grateful for in the present moment. This can be done by keeping a gratitude journal or simply taking a few moments each day to reflect on what you appreciate in your life.

Coping Strategy #6: Cultivating a Positive Mindset

Cultivating a positive mindset is another important coping strategy when facing adversity. It involves shifting your perspective and focusing on the positive aspects of your life. When you have a positive mindset, you are better able to handle challenges, bounce back from setbacks, and find solutions to problems.

The benefits of a positive mindset are numerous. It improves your mental and physical health, enhances your relationships, and increases your overall well-being. Research has shown that individuals with a positive mindset have better coping skills, higher levels of resilience, and greater life satisfaction.

Cultivating a positive mindset starts with becoming aware of your thoughts and beliefs. Notice when negative thoughts or self-limiting beliefs arise and challenge them. Replace negative thoughts with positive affirmations or realistic and empowering statements.

Practicing gratitude is another powerful way to cultivate a positive mindset. Gratitude involves focusing on what you appreciate in your life and expressing gratitude for it. This can be done through journaling, creating a gratitude jar, or simply taking a few moments each day to reflect on what you are grateful for.

Another practice is reframing, which involves looking at challenges from a different perspective. Instead of seeing them as obstacles, see them as opportunities for growth and learning. Look for the lessons or silver linings in difficult situations and focus on what you can control rather than what you can't.

Coping Strategy #7: Setting Realistic Goals and Taking Action

Setting realistic goals and taking action is another crucial coping strategy when facing adversity. Goals provide us with direction, motivation, and a sense of purpose. They give us something to strive for and help us stay focused during difficult times.

The importance of setting goals cannot be overstated. Research has shown that individuals who set goals are more likely to achieve them and have better mental health outcomes. Goals provide us with a sense of control and agency in the face of adversity.

When setting goals, it is important to make them realistic and achievable. Break them down into smaller, manageable steps and set deadlines for each step. This will help you stay motivated and track your progress.

Taking action is equally important as setting goals. It involves taking small, consistent steps towards your goals, even when faced with challenges or setbacks. Taking action helps build momentum and creates a sense of accomplishment, which can boost your confidence and resilience.

Coping Strategy #8: Seeking Professional Help and Therapy

Seeking professional help and therapy is another important coping strategy when facing adversity. Sometimes, the challenges we face are too overwhelming to handle on our own, and seeking professional support can make a significant difference in our well-being.

The benefits of seeking professional help are numerous. Therapists and counselors are trained to provide support, guidance, and evidence-based interventions to help individuals navigate through difficult times. They can help you gain insight into your thoughts, emotions, and behaviors and develop coping strategies that work for you.

Finding the right therapist is crucial in getting the support you need. Look for a therapist who specializes in the specific challenges you are facing or has experience working with individuals who have gone through similar experiences. It is also important to find someone you feel comfortable with and can trust.

There are different types of therapy available depending on your needs. Cognitive-behavioral therapy (CBT) focuses on identifying and changing negative thought patterns and behaviors. Acceptance and commitment therapy (ACT) focuses on accepting difficult emotions and taking action towards your values. Eye movement desensitization and reprocessing (EMDR) is a therapy specifically designed to help individuals process traumatic experiences.

Coping Strategy #9: Embracing Change and Adaptability

Embracing change and adaptability is another important coping strategy when facing adversity. Change is inevitable in life, and being able to adapt to new circumstances is crucial for our well-being and resilience.

The importance of embracing change cannot be overstated. Resisting or avoiding change can lead to increased stress, anxiety, and a sense of helplessness. On the other hand, embracing change allows us to grow, learn, and discover new possibilities.

Adaptability is the ability to adjust to new circumstances and navigate through challenges. It involves being open-minded, flexible, and willing to learn from new experiences. Adaptability allows us to find creative solutions to problems and make the most out of difficult situations.

There are different ways to develop adaptability. One way is through cultivating a growth mindset. A growth mindset is the belief that our abilities and intelligence can be developed through effort and learning. It involves embracing challenges, persisting in the face of setbacks, and seeing failures as opportunities for growth.

Another way is through practicing resilience. Resilience is the ability to bounce back from setbacks and adversity. It involves developing coping skills, building social support networks, and maintaining a positive mindset. Resilience can be cultivated through self-care, mindfulness, and seeking support when needed.

Coping Strategy #10: Learning from Failure and Resilience

Learning from failure and developing resilience is another important coping strategy when facing adversity. Failure is a natural part of life, and how we respond to it can make a significant difference in our well-being and success.

The benefits of learning from failure are numerous. Failure provides us with valuable lessons, insights, and opportunities for growth. It teaches us resilience, perseverance, and the importance of adaptability. By learning from failure, we can become stronger, wiser, and more resilient individuals.

Developing resilience is crucial in bouncing back from setbacks and adversity. Resilience involves the ability to recover quickly from difficulties and maintain a positive mindset in the face of challenges. It is not about avoiding or denying difficult emotions but rather about finding healthy ways to cope with them.

There are different ways to develop resilience. One way is through building a strong support system. Surround yourself with people who believe in you, support you, and provide you with emotional validation and practical assistance. Seek out mentors or role models who have overcome similar challenges and can provide guidance and inspiration.

Another way is through practicing self-care and mindfulness. Take care of your physical, emotional, and mental well-being. Engage in activities that bring you joy, reduce stress, and promote relaxation. Practice mindfulness to stay present and grounded in the midst of adversity.

Overcoming Adversity and Thriving in Life

In conclusion, coping strategies are essential tools that can help us navigate through adversity and overcome its challenges. They provide us with the skills and techniques to manage stress, regulate our emotions, and maintain our well-being. By implementing coping strategies in our lives, we can not only overcome adversity but also thrive and grow from it.

Understanding the impact of adversity on our mental and physical health is crucial in recognizing the importance of coping strategies. Adversity can take a toll on our well-being, leading to stress, anxiety, depression, and other mental health issues. Coping strategies provide us with the tools to manage these challenges and maintain our well-being.

The ten coping strategies discussed in this article - accepting the situation and your emotions, building a support system, practicing self-care and mindfulness, finding meaning and purpose in life, focusing on the present moment, cultivating a positive mindset, setting realistic goals and taking action, seeking professional help when needed, engaging in healthy distractions, and maintaining a sense of humor - can greatly contribute to one's ability to navigate difficult circumstances and maintain overall well-being. By implementing these strategies, individuals can develop resilience and effectively manage stress, ultimately leading to improved mental and emotional health. It is important to remember that coping strategies may vary from person to person, and it may take time to find the ones that work best for each individual. However, by actively seeking out and practicing these strategies, individuals can enhance their ability to cope with adversity and lead a more fulfilling life.

Chapter 19: The Different Types of Friendships and Why They Matter

Friendships play a crucial role in our mental and emotional well-being. They provide us with a sense of belonging, support, and companionship. Having a diverse group of friends can enrich our lives and help us grow as individuals. In this article, we will explore the different types of friendships and how each type serves a unique purpose in our lives.

The Different Types of Friendships: An Overview

Friendships come in various forms, each serving a different purpose in our lives. Some friendships are formed during childhood and last a lifetime, while others are made in the workplace or online. Each type of friendship brings its own set of benefits and challenges.

Childhood Friends: The Ones Who Know You Best

Childhood friends hold a special place in our hearts. They have known us since we were young and have witnessed our growth and development. These friends provide a sense of comfort and familiarity, as they know us better than anyone else. They understand our quirks, strengths, and weaknesses. Childhood friends often share memories and experiences that no one else can relate to.

Work Friends: The Ones Who Make the Day Go By Faster

Having friends in the workplace is essential for our overall well-being. Work friends can make the workday more enjoyable and less stressful.

They provide support during challenging times and celebrate our successes. Work friends also understand the unique challenges we face in our professional lives and can offer valuable advice and guidance.

Online Friends: The Ones Who Connect You to the World

With the rise of social media and online communities, online friendships have become increasingly common. Online friends can provide a sense of community and support, especially for those who may feel isolated or have difficulty forming connections in their physical surroundings. These friendships allow us to connect with people from different parts of the world, expanding our perspectives and understanding of different cultures.

Long-Distance Friends: The Ones Who Keep You Grounded

Maintaining long-distance friendships can be challenging, but they can also be incredibly rewarding. Long-distance friends provide a different perspective on life, as they may have different experiences and live in different environments. These friendships require effort and communication, but they can help us stay grounded and connected to our roots.

Acquaintances: The Ones Who Make Life Interesting

Acquaintances play an important role in our lives, even if we may not be as close to them as our closest friends. Acquaintances introduce us to new experiences and perspectives. They can expand our social circles and provide opportunities for personal and professional growth.

Acquaintances can also serve as a bridge between different social groups, bringing people together and fostering a sense of community.

Mentor Friends: The Ones Who Guide You Through Life

Having mentor friends is crucial for personal and professional development. These friends provide guidance, support, and advice based on their own experiences. Mentor friends can help us navigate through challenging situations, make important decisions, and achieve our goals. They offer a unique perspective and can serve as role models in our lives.

Casual Friends: The Ones Who Bring Joy to Your Life

Casual friends bring joy and spontaneity into our lives. These friendships are often based on shared interests or hobbies and provide an opportunity for fun and relaxation. Casual friends may not be as deeply involved in our lives as our closest friends, but they still play an important role in providing companionship and enjoyment.

Frenemies: The Ones Who Teach You About Boundaries

Dealing with frenemies can be challenging, but these relationships can teach us valuable lessons about setting boundaries and standing up for ourselves. Frenemies are individuals who may appear friendly on the surface but may have ulterior motives or engage in toxic behavior. Recognizing and navigating these relationships can help us develop a stronger sense of self and learn to prioritize our well-being.

The Value of Friendship in Our Lives

Friendships are an essential part of our lives. They provide us with support, companionship, and a sense of belonging. Having a diverse group of friends allows us to experience different perspectives, learn from others, and grow as individuals. Whether it's childhood friends, work friends, online friends, or mentor friends, each type of friendship serves a unique purpose and enriches our lives in its own way. So, cherish your friendships and invest time and effort into nurturing them.

Chapter 20: The Power of Embracing Your Unique Identity

Embracing your unique identity is crucial for living a fulfilling and authentic life. Each person is born with a set of qualities, characteristics, and experiences that make them different from anyone else. However, society often puts pressure on individuals to conform to certain norms and expectations, causing many people to suppress their true selves. This can lead to feelings of dissatisfaction, low self-esteem, and a lack of fulfillment. Embracing your unique identity allows you to fully express who you are, leading to a greater sense of self-acceptance and happiness.

Understanding Your Unique Identity: What Makes You Different

To embrace your unique identity, it is important to first understand what makes you different from others. This involves identifying your unique qualities, characteristics, and experiences. Take some time to reflect on your strengths and weaknesses, your passions and interests, and the values that guide your life. Consider the experiences that have shaped you and the lessons you have learned along the way. By understanding what makes you different, you can begin to appreciate and embrace those aspects of yourself.

The Benefits of Embracing Your Uniqueness: Improved Self-Esteem and Confidence

Embracing your uniqueness can have a profound impact on your self-esteem and confidence. When you fully accept and embrace who you are, you no longer feel the need to compare yourself to others or seek validation from external sources. Instead, you develop a deep sense of self-worth that comes from within. This newfound self-esteem and confidence can positively impact all areas of your life, from personal relationships to professional endeavors.

Overcoming Society's Pressure to Conform: Why It's Important to Be Yourself

Society often puts pressure on individuals to conform to certain norms and expectations. From a young age, we are bombarded with messages about how we should look, act, and think. This pressure to conform can be stifling and can cause individuals to suppress their true selves in order to fit in. However, it is important to remember that true happiness and fulfillment come from being yourself, not from trying to be someone you are not. By staying true to yourself, you not only honor your own unique identity but also inspire others to do the same.

The Dangers of Suppressing Your Unique Identity: Mental Health and Emotional Consequences

Suppressing your unique identity can have serious consequences for your mental health and emotional well-being. When you constantly suppress who you truly are, you may experience feelings of emptiness, dissatisfaction, and even depression. This can lead to a lack of self-confidence and a diminished sense of self-worth. Additionally, suppressing your unique identity can cause feelings of resentment and frustration, as you are denying yourself the opportunity to fully express who you are. It is important to prioritize your mental health and emotional well-being by embracing your unique identity.

Finding Your Voice: How to Express Your Authentic Self

Finding your voice and expressing your authentic self can be a challenging process, but it is essential for embracing your unique identity. Start by identifying what truly matters to you and what you are passionate about. Surround yourself with supportive people who encourage and uplift you. Practice self-reflection and journaling to explore your thoughts and feelings. Take small steps towards expressing your authentic self, whether it's through creative outlets, speaking up in conversations, or pursuing activities that align with your values. Remember that finding your voice is a lifelong journey, and it's okay to take it one step at a time.

Embracing Your Unique Identity in Relationships: Honesty and Vulnerability

Embracing your unique identity is crucial in building deep and meaningful relationships. Honesty and vulnerability are key components of authentic connections with others. By being honest about who you are and what you believe in, you attract people who appreciate and accept you for who you truly are. This leads to more fulfilling relationships built on trust and understanding. Embracing your unique identity also allows you to set boundaries and communicate your needs effectively, leading to healthier and more balanced relationships.

Navigating Professional Settings: How to Stand Out Without Compromising Your Identity

In professional settings, it can be challenging to stand out without compromising your unique identity. However, it is possible to maintain your authenticity while still excelling in your career. Start by identifying your strengths and leveraging them in your work. Find ways to incorporate your passions and interests into your professional life. Surround yourself with supportive colleagues who appreciate and value your unique contributions. Remember that being true to yourself is an asset, as it allows you to bring a fresh perspective and innovative ideas to the table.

Celebrating Diversity: The Importance of Accepting Others' Unique Identities

Embracing your own unique identity also involves accepting and celebrating the unique identities of others. Diversity is a beautiful aspect of humanity, and by embracing and accepting the differences in others, we create a more inclusive and accepting society. Take the time to learn about different cultures, beliefs, and experiences. Engage in conversations with people who have different perspectives than your own. By celebrating diversity, we can foster a sense of unity and create a world where everyone feels valued and accepted for who they are.

Overcoming Obstacles: How to Stay True to Yourself in the Face of Adversity

Staying true to yourself can be challenging, especially in the face of adversity. However, it is during these difficult times that embracing your unique identity becomes even more important. Surround yourself with a support system of friends, family, or mentors who uplift and encourage you. Practice self-care and prioritize your mental health. Develop resilience and perseverance by viewing challenges as opportunities for growth and learning. Remember that staying true to yourself is a lifelong journey, and it is okay to make mistakes along the way.

The Power of Embracing Your Unique Identity

and Living a Fulfilling Life

Embracing your unique identity is a powerful act that can lead to a more fulfilling and authentic life. By understanding and accepting what makes you different, you can develop a deep sense of self-worth and confidence. Embracing your uniqueness allows you to express your authentic self, leading to deeper connections in relationships and a greater sense of purpose in your professional life. By celebrating diversity and accepting others' unique identities, we create a more inclusive and accepting society. Embracing your unique identity is not always easy, but it is a journey worth taking for the sake of living a truly fulfilling life.

Chapter 21: The Science Behind Sensory Sensitivities: Understanding the Brain-Body Connection

Sensory sensitivities are a common experience for many individuals, yet they often go unnoticed or misunderstood. These sensitivities can have a significant impact on daily life, affecting everything from how we interact with our environment to our relationships with others. In this article, we will explore what sensory sensitivities are, how they are processed by the brain and body, and the various ways in which they can impact our lives. By understanding sensory sensitivities and their effects, we can work towards creating a more inclusive and supportive society for individuals who experience them.

What are sensory sensitivities?

Sensory sensitivities refer to an individual's heightened or exaggerated response to sensory stimuli. This means that certain sounds, sights, textures, tastes, or smells can be overwhelming or uncomfortable for someone with sensory sensitivities. While everyone has their own unique sensory preferences and aversions, individuals with sensory sensitivities experience these reactions to a much greater degree.

Examples of common sensory sensitivities include sensitivity to loud noises, such as sirens or fireworks, which can cause distress or anxiety. Some individuals may also be sensitive to certain textures, finding them uncomfortable or even painful to touch. Others may have heightened sensitivity to bright lights or strong smells, which can be overwhelming and cause discomfort.

The brain-body connection: How do they work together?

The brain and body work together in a complex process to process and interpret sensory information. This process is known as the sensory processing system. The sensory processing system involves the brain receiving information from the body's senses and then organizing and making sense of that information.

When we encounter a sensory stimulus, such as a loud noise or a soft touch, our sensory receptors send signals to the brain. The brain then processes these signals and determines how to respond. This response can vary depending on the individual's unique sensory profile and their past experiences with similar stimuli.

The role of the brain in sensory processing

The brain plays a crucial role in sensory processing. Different parts of the brain are responsible for processing and interpreting different types of sensory information. For example, the auditory cortex is responsible for processing sound, while the visual cortex processes visual information.

In addition to these specialized areas, there are also regions of the brain that integrate and make sense of the information from multiple senses. The parietal lobe, for example, helps to integrate information from the senses of touch, vision, and proprioception (the sense of body position and movement).

The brain processes sensory information by creating neural pathways that allow for the transmission of signals between different areas. These pathways help to organize and make sense of the sensory input, allowing us to understand and respond to our environment.

The impact of sensory sensitivities on daily life

Sensory sensitivities can have a significant impact on daily activities and routines. For example, someone with sensitivity to loud noises may find it difficult to concentrate in a noisy classroom or workplace. They may also experience anxiety or distress in crowded or noisy environments, such as shopping malls or concerts.

Sensory sensitivities can also impact social interactions and relationships. For example, someone with sensitivity to touch may find hugs or physical contact uncomfortable, which can make it challenging to navigate social situations. Additionally, individuals with sensory sensitivities may have difficulty filtering out irrelevant sensory information, making it harder to focus on conversations or engage in social activities.

Understanding the different types of sensory sensitivities

There are several different types of sensory sensitivities that individuals may experience. These include auditory sensitivities, visual sensitivities, tactile sensitivities, and olfactory sensitivities.

Auditory sensitivities refer to an individual's heightened sensitivity to sounds. This can include sensitivity to loud noises, certain frequencies, or specific types of sounds. Visual sensitivities involve a heightened response to visual stimuli, such as bright lights or busy visual environments. Tactile sensitivities refer to a heightened sensitivity to touch or textures, which can make certain fabrics or physical contact uncomfortable. Olfactory sensitivities involve a heightened sensitivity to smells, which can be overwhelming or unpleasant.

Each type of sensitivity can impact daily life in different ways. For example, auditory sensitivities can make it difficult to concentrate or participate in activities that involve loud noises, such as concerts or sporting events. Visual sensitivities can make it challenging to navigate visually stimulating environments, such as crowded streets or shopping malls. Tactile sensitivities can make it uncomfortable to wear certain fabrics or engage in physical contact. Olfactory sensitivities can make it difficult to tolerate certain smells, such as perfumes or cleaning products.

The link between sensory sensitivities and autism

Sensory sensitivities are highly prevalent in individuals with autism spectrum disorder (ASD). In fact, sensory sensitivities are one of the diagnostic criteria for ASD. Many individuals with ASD experience sensory sensitivities to a greater degree than the general population.

The link between sensory sensitivities and autism is not fully understood, but it is believed that differences in brain processing and connectivity may play a role. Individuals with ASD may have atypical neural responses to sensory stimuli, leading to heightened sensitivity or aversion.

Understanding the link between sensory sensitivities and autism is crucial for providing appropriate support and accommodations for individuals on the spectrum. By recognizing and addressing sensory sensitivities, we can help create environments that are more inclusive and supportive for individuals with ASD.

How sensory sensitivities can affect mental health

Sensory sensitivities can have a significant impact on mental health. Individuals with sensory sensitivities may experience increased levels of anxiety, stress, or depression due to their heightened response to sensory stimuli.

For example, someone with auditory sensitivities may feel anxious or overwhelmed in noisy environments, leading to increased stress levels. Similarly, someone with tactile sensitivities may experience anxiety or discomfort in situations that involve physical contact or certain textures.

Addressing sensory sensitivities is crucial for supporting mental health and well-being. By providing individuals with strategies and accommodations to manage their sensitivities, we can help reduce anxiety and stress levels, improving overall mental health outcomes.

The importance of early intervention for sensory sensitivities

Early intervention is crucial for managing sensory sensitivities and promoting positive outcomes. By identifying and addressing sensory sensitivities early on, individuals can develop coping strategies and receive appropriate support to manage their sensitivities.

Early intervention can involve a range of strategies, including sensory-based therapies, environmental modifications, and education for parents and caregivers. By implementing these interventions early in life, individuals can develop the skills and strategies needed to navigate their sensory sensitivities more effectively.

Research has shown that early intervention can lead to improved outcomes in individuals with sensory sensitivities. By addressing these sensitivities early on, individuals are better equipped to manage their sensitivities and participate fully in daily activities and routines.

The role of therapy in managing sensory sensitivities

Therapy plays a crucial role in managing sensory sensitivities. Occupational therapy (OT) is often used to help individuals develop skills and strategies to manage their sensitivities. OT focuses on improving an individual's ability to participate in daily activities by addressing sensory processing difficulties.

Sensory integration therapy is another type of therapy that can be beneficial for individuals with sensory sensitivities. This therapy involves engaging in activities that provide controlled sensory input to help regulate the individual's response to stimuli.

Therapy can help individuals with sensory sensitivities develop coping strategies, improve self-regulation skills, and increase their tolerance for sensory stimuli. By working with a therapist, individuals can learn how to navigate their sensitivities more effectively and participate fully in daily life.

Strategies for coping with sensory sensitivities

There are several strategies that individuals with sensory sensitivities can use to cope with their sensitivities. One common strategy is the use of a sensory diet, which involves engaging in specific activities or exercises to provide the individual with the sensory input they need to regulate their response to stimuli.

Environmental modifications can also be helpful in managing sensory sensitivities. This can involve creating a calm and quiet space at home or in the workplace, using noise-cancelling headphones or earplugs, or adjusting lighting levels to reduce visual stimulation.

Other strategies for coping with sensory sensitivities include deep pressure techniques, such as weighted blankets or compression garments, and mindfulness or relaxation exercises to help manage anxiety or stress.

By implementing these strategies, individuals can better manage their sensitivities and participate more fully in daily activities and routines.

The future of research in sensory processing disorders

Research in sensory processing disorders is an active and evolving field. There is still much to learn about the underlying mechanisms of sensory sensitivities and how they impact individuals' lives.

Current research is focused on understanding the neural basis of sensory processing disorders, identifying effective interventions and therapies, and developing tools for assessing and diagnosing sensory sensitivities.

Future research may explore the genetic and environmental factors that contribute to sensory sensitivities, as well as the long-term outcomes for individuals with sensory processing disorders. Additionally, there is a growing interest in understanding the intersection between sensory sensitivities and other neurodevelopmental conditions, such as ADHD or anxiety disorders.

By continuing to invest in research on sensory processing disorders, we can gain a better understanding of these conditions and develop more effective interventions and supports for individuals who experience sensory sensitivities.

Sensory sensitivities are a common experience for many individuals and can have a significant impact on daily life. By understanding the nature of sensory sensitivities, how they are processed by the brain and body, and their effects on mental health and well-being, we can work towards creating a more inclusive and supportive society.

Early intervention and therapy play a crucial role in managing sensory sensitivities and promoting positive outcomes. By providing individuals with the tools and strategies they need to navigate their sensitivities, we can help them participate fully in daily activities and routines.

It is important to continue investing in research on sensory processing disorders to further our understanding of these conditions and develop more effective interventions and supports. By increasing awareness and understanding of sensory sensitivities, we can create a more inclusive and supportive society for individuals who experience them.

Chapter 22: The Meaning Behind Common Dream Symbols and Interpretations

Dreams have fascinated humans for centuries. They have been the subject of countless studies, theories, and interpretations. Dreams have the power to transport us to another world, where our subconscious thoughts and emotions come to life. They can provide insight into our deepest desires, fears, and aspirations. Understanding the importance of dreams and how they can reveal hidden aspects of ourselves is crucial for personal growth and self-awareness.

Dreams are a window into our subconscious mind. While we are awake, our conscious mind is busy with daily tasks and responsibilities, but when we sleep, our subconscious takes over. Dreams can be seen as a way for our subconscious to communicate with us, bringing to the surface thoughts and emotions that we may not be aware of in our waking life. By paying attention to our dreams and analyzing their symbols and meanings, we can gain a deeper understanding of ourselves and our inner world.

Dream Symbols: Why They Matter

Dream symbols play a significant role in understanding the meaning behind our dreams. These symbols can hold deep meaning and provide insight into our subconscious thoughts and emotions. They can be objects, people, or actions that appear in our dreams and carry a symbolic representation.

Identifying and interpreting dream symbols is essential for understanding the messages that our subconscious is trying to convey. For example, if you dream about water, it could represent emotions and the unconscious mind. If you dream about flying, it could symbolize freedom and control. By recognizing these symbols and their meanings, we can gain valuable insights into ourselves and our inner world.

Water: Symbolism and Interpretations

Water is a common symbol that appears in many dreams. It can have various interpretations depending on the context of the dream. Water often represents emotions and the unconscious mind. The state of the water in your dream can provide further insight into your emotional state.

For example, calm and clear water may indicate a sense of peace and tranquility, while turbulent and murky water may suggest emotional turmoil or unresolved issues. Drowning in water could symbolize being overwhelmed by emotions, while swimming in water could represent a sense of control and adaptability.

Understanding the symbolism of water in your dreams can help you gain a deeper understanding of your emotional state and the underlying issues that may need to be addressed.

Flying: What It Means in Your Dreams

Flying is a common dream symbol that often represents freedom and control. When we dream about flying, it can evoke feelings of liberation and empowerment. Flying dreams can also symbolize a desire to escape from a challenging situation or to rise above obstacles in our waking life.

The interpretation of flying dreams can vary depending on the context and emotions associated with the dream. For example, if you feel joy and exhilaration while flying, it may indicate a sense of freedom and empowerment. On the other hand, if you feel fear or anxiety while flying, it could suggest a fear of losing control or a lack of confidence in your abilities.

By exploring the symbolism and emotions associated with flying dreams, you can gain insight into your desires for freedom and control in your waking life.

Teeth: The Hidden Meaning Behind This Common Dream Symbol

Dreams about teeth are incredibly common and can hold significant meaning. Teeth often represent anxiety and powerlessness. They can symbolize our fears of losing control or our concerns about our appearance and how others perceive us.

Different interpretations of teeth dreams can provide insight into specific aspects of our lives. For example, dreaming about losing teeth may suggest feelings of powerlessness or a fear of aging. Dreaming about broken or decayed teeth could symbolize insecurities or concerns about our physical appearance.

By paying attention to the symbolism and emotions associated with teeth dreams, we can gain a deeper understanding of our anxieties and insecurities.

Falling: Decoding the Symbolism of Falling in Dreams

Dreams about falling are another common experience that can hold deep symbolism. Falling dreams often represent insecurity and a fear of failure. They can reflect our anxieties about losing control or our concerns about not being able to meet expectations.

Interpreting falling dreams requires examining the emotions and context of the dream. For example, if you feel fear or panic while falling, it may suggest a lack of confidence or a fear of not being able to handle a situation. If you feel a sense of surrender or acceptance while falling, it could indicate a willingness to let go and trust the process.

By exploring the symbolism and emotions associated with falling dreams, we can gain insight into our fears and insecurities and work towards overcoming them.

Animals: What They Represent in Your Dreams

Animals are frequent visitors in our dreams and can hold various meanings depending on the animal and its behavior. Animals often represent different aspects of ourselves or specific qualities that we associate with them.

For example, dreaming about a lion may symbolize strength, courage, or leadership, while dreaming about a snake could represent transformation or hidden fears. The behavior of the animal in your dream can also provide further insight into its meaning. For instance, if the animal is aggressive or threatening, it may suggest repressed anger or unresolved conflicts.

By paying attention to the animals in your dreams and their behaviors, you can gain a deeper understanding of your own qualities and emotions.

Death: The Deeper Significance of Dreaming About Death

Dreams about death can be unsettling but often carry profound symbolism. Death in dreams rarely represents literal death but rather signifies change and transformation. It can symbolize the end of one phase of life and the beginning of another.

Interpreting death dreams requires examining the emotions and context of the dream. For example, if you dream about your own death but feel peaceful or accepting, it may suggest a willingness to let go of old patterns or beliefs. If you dream about the death of a loved one and feel grief or sadness, it could indicate unresolved emotions or a fear of loss.

By exploring the symbolism and emotions associated with death dreams, we can gain insight into our fears, desires for change, and our ability to adapt and grow.

Nakedness: The Meaning Behind Dreams of Being Naked in Public

Dreams of being naked in public are incredibly common and can evoke feelings of vulnerability and shame. These dreams often represent our fears of being exposed or judged by others. They can reflect our insecurities about our physical appearance or our concerns about being seen for who we truly are.

Interpreting nakedness dreams requires examining the emotions and context of the dream. For example, if you feel embarrassed or humiliated while being naked in public, it may suggest a fear of being judged or a lack of self-confidence. If you feel comfortable and unashamed, it could indicate a sense of self-acceptance and authenticity.

By exploring the symbolism and emotions associated with nakedness dreams, we can gain insight into our insecurities, fears, and our journey towards self-acceptance.

Dreams of Being Chased: What Your Subconscious Mind is Trying to Tell You

Dreams of being chased are incredibly common and often reflect our subconscious fears and anxieties. Being chased in a dream can symbolize avoidance and fear. It may represent unresolved issues or situations that we are trying to escape from in our waking life.

Interpreting being chased dreams requires examining the emotions and context of the dream. For example, if you feel fear or panic while being chased, it may suggest a fear of confronting a particular situation or a desire to avoid responsibility. If you feel excitement or exhilaration while being chased, it could indicate a desire for adventure or a need for change.

By exploring the symbolism and emotions associated with being chased dreams, we can gain insight into our fears, desires, and the areas of our lives that may need attention.

Using Dream Interpretation to Unlock Your Inner World

Dream interpretation is a powerful tool for personal growth and self-awareness. By understanding the importance of dreams and their symbolism, we can gain valuable insights into our subconscious thoughts and emotions. Dreams provide a window into our inner world, revealing hidden desires, fears, and aspirations.

By exploring and analyzing our dreams, we can uncover patterns, identify unresolved issues, and gain a deeper understanding of ourselves. Dream interpretation allows us to tap into our subconscious mind and use the wisdom it offers to navigate our waking life with greater clarity and purpose.

So next time you wake up from a dream, take a moment to reflect on its symbols and meanings. Pay attention to the emotions it evokes and the messages it may be trying to convey. By embracing the power of dreams and using dream interpretation as a tool for self-discovery, you can unlock the hidden depths of your inner world and embark on a journey of personal growth and self-awareness.

Chapter 23: The Power of Persistence: How These 25 Achievers Overcame Obstacles to Succeed

Persistence is defined as the quality of continuing to do something despite difficulties or opposition. It is an essential trait that plays a crucial role in achieving success. Without persistence, it is easy to give up when faced with challenges or setbacks. However, those who persist despite obstacles are more likely to reach their goals and achieve success.

There are numerous examples of successful individuals who have demonstrated persistence in their journey towards success. One such example is Thomas Edison, the inventor of the light bulb. Edison famously said, "I have not failed. I've just found 10,000 ways that won't work." Despite facing countless failures and setbacks, Edison persisted and eventually succeeded in creating a practical and commercially viable light bulb.

Another example is J.K. Rowling, the author of the Harry Potter series. Rowling faced numerous rejections from publishers before finally finding one who believed in her work. Her persistence paid off, and she went on to become one of the most successful authors of all time.

These examples highlight the importance of persistence in achieving success. Without persistence, Edison may have given up on his invention, and Rowling may have abandoned her dream of becoming a published author. Persistence allows individuals to overcome challenges and continue working towards their goals, even when the odds are stacked against them.

Overcoming Adversity: Stories of Resilience and Determination

There are countless stories of individuals who have overcome adversity through persistence and determination. One such story is that of Oprah Winfrey. Winfrey faced a difficult childhood marked by poverty and abuse. However, she persisted and went on to become one of the most influential media personalities in the world.

Another inspiring story is that of Nelson Mandela. Mandela spent 27 years in prison for his anti-apartheid activism. Despite the hardships he faced, Mandela never gave up on his fight for equality and justice. His persistence eventually led to the end of apartheid and his election as the first black president of South Africa.

These stories teach us valuable lessons about resilience and determination. They show us that no matter how difficult our circumstances may be, we have the power to overcome them through persistence. They remind us that setbacks and challenges are not the end of the road, but rather opportunities for growth and transformation.

The Role of Failure in Building Resilience and Perseverance

Failure is often seen as a negative outcome, but it can actually be a stepping stone to success. Many successful individuals have experienced failure before achieving their goals. For example, Steve Jobs was famously fired from Apple, the company he co-founded. However, he persisted and went on to return to Apple and transform it into one of the most valuable companies in the world.

Failure teaches us valuable lessons and helps us build resilience and perseverance. It forces us to reevaluate our approach, learn from our mistakes, and try again. Without failure, we would not have the opportunity to grow and improve.

The Power of Positive Thinking: How Optimism Can Fuel Persistence

Positive thinking plays a crucial role in fueling persistence. When we approach challenges with a positive mindset, we are more likely to persevere and find solutions. Positive thinking helps us maintain a sense of optimism and belief in ourselves, even when faced with difficulties.

Cultivating a positive mindset involves focusing on the good in every situation, practicing gratitude, and reframing negative thoughts into positive ones. It also involves surrounding ourselves with positive influences and avoiding negativity.

The Importance of Goal-Setting and Planning in Achieving Success

Setting goals and making plans is essential for persistence. Without clear goals, it is easy to lose focus and motivation. Goals provide us with a sense of direction and purpose, and they help us stay on track when faced with challenges.

Effective goal-setting involves setting specific, measurable, achievable, relevant, and time-bound (SMART) goals. It also involves breaking down larger goals into smaller, manageable tasks. Planning is equally important, as it helps us create a roadmap for achieving our goals and allows us to anticipate and overcome obstacles.

The Benefits of Consistency and Discipline in Pursuing Goals

Consistency and discipline are key to achieving success. Consistency involves taking small, consistent actions towards our goals every day. It is about showing up and putting in the work, even when we don't feel like it.

Discipline is the ability to stay focused and committed to our goals, even when faced with distractions or temptations. It involves making sacrifices and prioritizing our goals over short-term gratification.

Consistency and discipline help us build momentum and make progress towards our goals. They also help us develop good habits and overcome procrastination.

The Role of Support Systems in Encouraging Persistence

Having a support system can greatly enhance our ability to persist. A support system consists of individuals who believe in us, encourage us, and provide emotional support during challenging times.

A strong support system can provide us with motivation, accountability, and guidance. They can offer advice, share their own experiences, and help us navigate obstacles. They can also provide a listening ear and offer words of encouragement when we feel discouraged.

Building a strong support system involves surrounding ourselves with positive and supportive individuals. It may involve seeking out mentors or joining communities of like-minded individuals who share similar goals and values.

The Impact of Perseverance on Personal Growth and Development

Persistence has a profound impact on personal growth and development. When we persist despite challenges, we develop resilience, determination, and self-confidence. We learn valuable lessons from our failures and setbacks, which help us grow and improve.

Persistence also allows us to push past our comfort zones and discover our true potential. It helps us develop new skills, overcome fears, and achieve things we never thought possible. It is through persistence that we can truly unlock our full potential and become the best version of ourselves.

The Connection Between Persistence and Success in Business

Persistence is particularly important in the world of business. Starting and running a successful business requires perseverance and the ability to overcome numerous challenges and setbacks.

Many successful businesses were built through persistence. For example, Amazon faced numerous challenges in its early years, but founder Jeff Bezos persisted and continued to innovate and expand. Today, Amazon is one of the largest companies in the world.

Persistence in business involves staying focused on long-term goals, adapting to changing circumstances, and continuously learning and improving. It also involves taking calculated risks and being willing to fail and learn from those failures.

The Lessons We Can Learn from These 25 Achievers

There are countless stories of successful individuals who persisted to achieve their dreams. Here are 25 examples:

1. Thomas Edison - Persistence in the face of failure
2. J.K. Rowling - Persistence in the face of rejection
3. Oprah Winfrey - Persistence in the face of adversity
4. Nelson Mandela - Persistence in the face of injustice
5. Steve Jobs - Persistence in the face of setbacks
6. Elon Musk - Persistence in the face of criticism
7. Serena Williams - Persistence in the face of obstacles
8. Walt Disney - Persistence in the face of bankruptcy
9. Michael Jordan - Persistence in the face of failure

10. Mark Zuckerberg - Persistence in the face of challenges
11. Bill Gates - Persistence in the face of competition
12. Malala Yousafzai - Persistence in the face of oppression
13. Warren Buffett - Persistence in the face of market fluctuations
14. Richard Branson - Persistence in the face of risk
15. Maya Angelou - Persistence in the face of discrimination
16. Stephen King - Persistence in the face of rejection
17. Henry Ford - Persistence in the face of skepticism
18. Coco Chanel - Persistence in the face of gender barriers
19. Muhammad Ali - Persistence in the face of adversity
20. Marie Curie - Persistence in the face of prejudice
21. Vincent Van Gogh - Persistence in the face of mental illness
22. Amelia Earhart - Persistence in the face of gender stereotypes
23. Mahatma Gandhi - Persistence in the face of resistance
24. Martin Luther King Jr. - Persistence in the face of opposition
25. Mother Teresa - Persistence in the face of poverty

From these achievers, we can learn the importance of persistence, resilience, determination, and positive thinking. We can learn that success is not achieved overnight, but rather through consistent effort and a refusal to give up.

Embracing Persistence as a Key to Achieving Your Dreams

In conclusion, persistence is a crucial trait that plays a significant role in achieving success. It allows individuals to overcome challenges, learn from failures, and continue working towards their goals despite setbacks.

By embracing persistence, we can unlock our full potential and achieve our dreams. It requires resilience, determination, positive thinking, goal-setting, planning, consistency, discipline, and a strong support system.

So, let us embrace persistence and commit to never giving up on our dreams. Let us remember the stories of those who persisted and achieved greatness against all odds. And let us believe in ourselves and our ability to overcome any challenge that comes our way. With persistence as our ally, there is no limit to what we can achieve.

Chapter 24: The Science of Resilience: Understanding the Biology Behind Our Ability to Adapt

Resilience is the ability to bounce back and adapt in the face of adversity, trauma, or stress. It is the capacity to recover quickly from difficult experiences and setbacks, and to maintain a positive outlook despite challenging circumstances. Resilience is not about avoiding or denying pain and hardship, but rather about facing them head-on and finding ways to navigate through them.

Resilience is an essential skill in everyday life because it helps us cope with the inevitable ups and downs that we all experience. Whether it's dealing with a breakup, losing a job, or facing a global pandemic, resilience allows us to maintain our mental and emotional well-being in the face of adversity. It helps us stay focused, motivated, and optimistic, even when things seem bleak.

The Brain's Role in Resilience: How the Brain Helps Us Adapt to Stressful Situations

The prefrontal cortex plays a crucial role in resilience. This part of the brain is responsible for executive functions such as decision-making, problem-solving, and emotional regulation. When faced with a stressful situation, the prefrontal cortex helps us assess the situation, make rational decisions, and regulate our emotions.

Neuroplasticity is another key factor in resilience. It refers to the brain's ability to reorganize itself by forming new neural connections throughout life. This means that our brains are not fixed entities but are constantly changing and adapting based on our experiences. Neuroplasticity allows us to learn from difficult experiences, develop new coping strategies, and build resilience over time.

The Stress Response: Understanding How Our Bodies React to Stress

The fight or flight response is a physiological reaction that occurs when we perceive a threat or danger. It triggers a cascade of hormonal and physiological changes in our bodies, preparing us to either fight the threat or flee from it. This response is essential for our survival in acute, life-threatening situations.

However, chronic stress can have detrimental effects on our bodies. When we are constantly exposed to stressors without adequate time to recover, our bodies remain in a state of heightened arousal. This can lead to a range of physical and mental health problems, including cardiovascular disease, weakened immune function, and anxiety disorders.

The Role of Hormones: How Hormones Affect Our Ability to Cope with Stress

Cortisol and adrenaline are two hormones that play a crucial role in the stress response. Cortisol helps regulate our energy levels, metabolism, and immune function, while adrenaline increases our heart rate and blood pressure, preparing us for action. In acute stress situations, these hormones are released to help us respond effectively.

However, chronic stress can disrupt the delicate balance of these hormones. Prolonged exposure to stress can lead to elevated cortisol levels, which can impair immune function, increase inflammation, and contribute to the development of chronic diseases such as diabetes and depression. It can also lead to adrenal fatigue, where the body's ability to produce cortisol becomes compromised.

The Immune System's Role in Resilience: How Our Body's Defenses Help Us Adapt

Stress has a significant impact on the immune system. While acute stress can temporarily enhance immune function, chronic stress can weaken it. When we are under prolonged stress, our bodies produce higher levels of pro-inflammatory cytokines, which can lead to chronic inflammation. This inflammation has been linked to a range of health problems, including autoimmune diseases and mental health disorders.

On the other hand, resilience can help protect and strengthen the immune system. Research has shown that individuals with higher levels of resilience have better immune function and are less susceptible to infections and diseases. Building resilience through various strategies can therefore have a positive impact on our overall health and well-being.

Genetics and Resilience: How Our Genes Affect Our Ability to Bounce Back

Genetic factors play a role in determining our resilience levels. Some individuals may be genetically predisposed to be more resilient, while others may be more susceptible to stress and adversity. Research has identified specific genes that are associated with resilience, such as those involved in the regulation of stress hormones and neurotransmitters.

However, it is important to note that genetics is not the sole determinant of resilience. Environmental factors and experiences also play a significant role in shaping our ability to cope with stress and bounce back from adversity. This is where the concept of epigenetics comes into play.

Epigenetics refers to the study of how environmental factors can influence gene expression without changing the underlying DNA sequence. It suggests that our experiences and the environments we are exposed to can modify the way our genes are expressed. This means that even if we have genetic predispositions for lower resilience, we can still build resilience through positive experiences and supportive environments.

Childhood Experiences and Resilience: How Early Life Events Shape Our Ability to Cope

Childhood experiences have a profound impact on our ability to develop resilience. Adverse childhood experiences, such as abuse, neglect, or household dysfunction, can have long-lasting effects on our physical and mental health. They can disrupt the development of key brain regions involved in emotional regulation and stress response, making individuals more vulnerable to stress and less resilient.

On the other hand, positive childhood experiences can help build resilience. Supportive relationships with caregivers, access to education and resources, and opportunities for personal growth and development can all contribute to the development of resilience in children. These positive experiences provide a buffer against adversity and help children develop the skills and mindset necessary to navigate through life's challenges.

Resilience and Mental Health: How Resilience Can Help Protect Against Mental Illness

Resilience plays a crucial role in protecting against mental illness. Research has shown that individuals with higher levels of resilience are less likely to develop mental health disorders such as depression, anxiety, and post-traumatic stress disorder (PTSD). They are better able to cope with stress, regulate their emotions, and maintain a positive outlook on life.

Furthermore, resilience can also help individuals recover from mental illness. It provides a foundation for individuals to bounce back from setbacks, learn from their experiences, and develop new coping strategies. Building resilience through therapy, support groups, and self-care practices can therefore be an effective way to manage and overcome mental health challenges.

Strategies for Building Resilience: Practical Tips for Strengthening Your Ability to Adapt

There are several strategies that can help individuals build resilience and strengthen their ability to adapt in the face of adversity. Mindfulness and meditation practices have been shown to reduce stress, improve emotional regulation, and enhance overall well-being. These practices involve paying attention to the present moment without judgment and cultivating a sense of acceptance and compassion.

Exercise and physical activity are also important for building resilience. Regular exercise has been shown to reduce stress, improve mood, and enhance cognitive function. It helps release endorphins, which are natural mood-boosting chemicals in the brain. Engaging in activities that you enjoy and that challenge you physically can help build physical and mental resilience.

Building social connections is another key strategy for building resilience. Having a strong support network of family, friends, and community members can provide emotional support, practical assistance, and a sense of belonging. Social connections help us feel valued and supported, which in turn enhances our ability to cope with stress and adversity.

The Importance of Social Support: How Relationships Help Us Build Resilience

Social support plays a crucial role in building resilience. Research has consistently shown that individuals with strong social connections are more resilient and better able to cope with stress. Having someone to talk to, share experiences with, and seek advice from can provide a sense of comfort and reassurance during difficult times.

Furthermore, social support can also help individuals develop new perspectives and coping strategies. By interacting with others who have faced similar challenges, we can learn from their experiences and gain new insights into our own situations. Social support can also provide a sense of accountability and motivation, as we are more likely to take action and make positive changes when we have the support of others.

Community support is also important for building resilience. Being part of a community that shares common values, goals, and interests can provide a sense of belonging and purpose. It can also provide opportunities for collaboration, learning, and personal growth. Community involvement allows individuals to contribute to something larger than themselves and make a positive impact on others, which can enhance their sense of resilience.

How Understanding the Science of Resilience Can Help Us Thrive in the Face of Adversity

Resilience is an essential skill that helps us navigate through life's challenges and maintain our mental and emotional well-being. Understanding the science behind resilience can provide us with valuable insights into how our brains, bodies, and relationships contribute to our ability to adapt and bounce back from adversity.

By building resilience through various strategies such as mindfulness, exercise, and social connections, we can enhance our ability to cope with stress and thrive in the face of adversity. Resilience is not something that we are born with or without; it is a skill that can be developed and strengthened over time.

By cultivating resilience, we can face life's challenges with confidence, optimism, and a sense of purpose. We can learn from our experiences, grow from setbacks, and emerge stronger and more resilient than ever before. Resilience is not about avoiding or denying pain; it is about embracing it, learning from it, and using it as fuel for personal growth and transformation.

Chapter 25: From Data to Wisdom: How to Turn 27 Insights into Actionable Knowledge

In today's world, data analysis has become an essential tool for businesses to make informed decisions. With the vast amount of data available, it is crucial for organizations to analyze and interpret this data to gain valuable insights. Data analysis allows businesses to identify patterns, trends, and correlations that can help them understand customer behavior, market trends, and other important factors that impact their operations.

Data analysis provides businesses with the ability to make data-driven decisions, rather than relying on intuition or guesswork. By analyzing data, businesses can uncover hidden patterns and trends that may not be immediately apparent. This allows them to make more accurate predictions and forecasts, which can ultimately lead to better decision-making and improved business outcomes.

Defining the Difference between Data, Information, and Knowledge

To understand the importance of data analysis, it is essential to first define the terms data, information, and knowledge and understand how they are related.

Data refers to raw facts or figures that are collected and stored. It can be in the form of numbers, text, images, or any other format. Data by itself does not have any meaning or context; it is simply a collection of information.

Information is derived from data through the process of organizing, analyzing, and interpreting it. It provides context and meaning to the raw data. Information helps businesses understand what the data is telling them and enables them to make informed decisions based on this understanding.

Knowledge goes a step further than information. It is the understanding gained from analyzing and interpreting information. Knowledge is the result of applying expertise and experience to the information derived from data analysis. It allows businesses to gain insights and make informed decisions based on their understanding of the data.

Understanding the difference between these terms is crucial because it helps businesses recognize that data alone is not enough; it needs to be transformed into meaningful information and knowledge through analysis and interpretation.

The Role of Insights in Turning Data into Wisdom

Insights are the valuable nuggets of information that can be derived from data analysis. They are the key to turning data into wisdom. Insights provide businesses with a deeper understanding of their operations, customers, and market trends.

Insights can be derived from data analysis by identifying patterns, trends, and correlations. By analyzing large datasets, businesses can uncover hidden relationships and gain a better understanding of cause and effect. For example, by analyzing customer purchase data, a business may discover that customers who buy product A are more likely to also buy product B. This insight can then be used to develop targeted marketing campaigns or cross-selling strategies.

Insights can also be used to make informed decisions. By understanding the implications of the data analysis, businesses can make better decisions that are based on evidence rather than intuition. For example, if data analysis reveals a decline in customer satisfaction, a business can take proactive measures to address the underlying issues and improve customer experience.

The Importance of Data Collection and Analysis Techniques

Data collection is the first step in the data analysis process. It involves gathering accurate and relevant data that is necessary for making informed decisions. Collecting accurate data is crucial because inaccurate or incomplete data can lead to incorrect conclusions and poor decision-making.

There are various techniques used in data analysis to extract insights from the collected data. These techniques include statistical analysis, data mining, machine learning, and predictive modeling. Statistical analysis involves using mathematical formulas and techniques to analyze and interpret data. Data mining involves discovering patterns and relationships in large datasets. Machine learning uses algorithms to automatically learn from data and make predictions or decisions. Predictive modeling involves creating models based on historical data to predict future outcomes.

The choice of data analysis technique depends on the nature of the data and the specific goals of the analysis. Each technique has its strengths and limitations, and businesses need to carefully select the appropriate technique based on their requirements.

Understanding the Different Types of Data and Their Significance

Data can be classified into different types based on its nature and characteristics. The two main types of data are quantitative data and qualitative data.

Quantitative data refers to numerical data that can be measured and analyzed using mathematical and statistical techniques. It includes data such as sales figures, customer demographics, and website traffic. Quantitative data is objective and can be easily analyzed to identify patterns and trends.

Qualitative data, on the other hand, refers to non-numerical data that provides insights into the opinions, attitudes, and behaviors of individuals or groups. It includes data such as customer feedback, survey responses, and interview transcripts. Qualitative data is subjective and requires a more interpretive approach to analysis.

Both quantitative and qualitative data are important for businesses. Quantitative data provides objective insights into customer behavior and market trends, while qualitative data provides a deeper understanding of customer preferences and motivations. By analyzing both types of data together, businesses can gain a more comprehensive understanding of their operations and make more informed decisions.

The Role of Visualization in Making Data More Understandable

Data visualization plays a crucial role in making data more understandable and accessible. It involves representing data in visual formats such as charts, graphs, and maps. By presenting data visually, businesses can quickly grasp patterns, trends, and relationships that may not be immediately apparent in raw data.

Data visualization helps businesses communicate complex information in a clear and concise manner. It allows decision-makers to quickly absorb information and make informed decisions based on their understanding of the visual representation of the data. For example, a line chart showing sales trends over time can help businesses identify seasonal patterns or changes in customer demand.

Visualization also enables businesses to explore data interactively. By using interactive visualizations, users can drill down into the data, filter it based on specific criteria, and explore different perspectives.

This allows businesses to gain deeper insights and make more informed decisions.

Identifying Patterns and Trends in Data Analysis

Identifying patterns and trends is a crucial step in data analysis. By analyzing large datasets, businesses can uncover hidden relationships and gain a better understanding of cause and effect. This can help them make more accurate predictions and forecasts, which can ultimately lead to better decision-making.

Patterns can be identified by analyzing the frequency and distribution of data values. For example, by analyzing customer purchase data, a business may discover that certain products are frequently purchased together. This insight can then be used to develop targeted marketing campaigns or cross-selling strategies.

Trends, on the other hand, refer to the direction and magnitude of change over time. By analyzing historical data, businesses can identify trends and make predictions about future outcomes. For example, by analyzing sales data over several years, a business may identify a gradual increase in demand for a particular product. This insight can then be used to plan production and inventory levels.

Identifying patterns and trends in data analysis is important because it allows businesses to anticipate changes and take proactive measures. By understanding the underlying patterns and trends, businesses can make more informed decisions that are based on evidence rather than intuition.

The Importance of Data Interpretation and Contextualization

Data interpretation is the process of making sense of the data by assigning meaning to it. It involves analyzing the data in the right context and drawing conclusions based on the analysis.

Interpreting data in the right context is crucial because data alone can be misleading. Without proper interpretation, businesses may draw incorrect conclusions or make poor decisions based on incomplete or biased information.

Contextualization involves considering the broader context in which the data was collected. This includes factors such as the purpose of the analysis, the specific goals of the business, and the external factors that may influence the data. By considering these factors, businesses can ensure that their interpretation of the data is accurate and relevant.

Data interpretation and contextualization are important because they help businesses make informed decisions based on a comprehensive understanding of the data. By interpreting the data in the right context, businesses can avoid making decisions based on incomplete or biased information and ensure that their decisions are based on evidence and facts.

Applying Data to Real-World Scenarios

Data analysis can be applied to a wide range of real-world scenarios to help businesses make informed decisions. Here are a few examples of how businesses have used data analysis to improve their operations:

1. Customer segmentation: By analyzing customer data, businesses can identify different segments of customers with similar characteristics and preferences. This allows them to develop targeted marketing campaigns and personalized offers that are more likely to resonate with each segment.

2. Supply chain optimization: By analyzing supply chain data, businesses can identify bottlenecks, inefficiencies, and areas for improvement. This allows them to optimize their supply chain operations, reduce costs, and improve customer satisfaction.

3. Fraud detection: By analyzing transaction data, businesses can identify patterns and anomalies that may indicate fraudulent activity.

This allows them to take proactive measures to prevent fraud and protect their assets.

4. Predictive maintenance: By analyzing equipment sensor data, businesses can predict when equipment is likely to fail and schedule maintenance activities accordingly. This helps prevent unplanned downtime and reduces maintenance costs.

These are just a few examples of how data analysis can be applied to real-world scenarios. The possibilities are endless, and businesses that embrace data analysis have a competitive advantage in today's data-driven world.

The Role of Machine Learning and Artificial Intelligence in Data Analysis

Machine learning and artificial intelligence (AI) play a crucial role in data analysis. These technologies enable businesses to analyze large datasets quickly and accurately, uncover hidden patterns and trends, and make predictions or decisions based on the analysis.

Machine learning algorithms can automatically learn from data and make predictions or decisions without being explicitly programmed. They can analyze large datasets and identify patterns and relationships that may not be immediately apparent to humans. This allows businesses to gain deeper insights and make more accurate predictions.

Artificial intelligence, on the other hand, refers to the broader field of computer science that focuses on creating intelligent machines that can perform tasks that would typically require human intelligence. AI techniques, such as natural language processing and image recognition, can be used to analyze unstructured data, such as text or images, and extract valuable insights.

Machine learning and artificial intelligence are particularly useful when dealing with big data, which refers to datasets that are too large or complex to be analyzed using traditional data analysis techniques.

These technologies enable businesses to process and analyze big data quickly and accurately, allowing them to gain valuable insights and make informed decisions.

Turning Insights into Actionable Wisdom

In conclusion, data analysis plays a crucial role in helping businesses make informed decisions. By analyzing and interpreting data, businesses can gain valuable insights that can be used to improve their operations, understand customer behavior, and identify market trends.

Insights derived from data analysis provide businesses with a deeper understanding of their operations and enable them to make more accurate predictions and forecasts. By turning insights into actionable wisdom, businesses can take proactive measures to address issues, optimize their operations, and improve their overall performance.

Data analysis techniques, such as statistical analysis, data mining, machine learning, and predictive modeling, enable businesses to extract insights from large datasets quickly and accurately. By analyzing both quantitative and qualitative data together and visualizing the results, businesses can gain a comprehensive understanding of their operations and make more informed decisions.

In today's data-driven world, businesses that embrace data analysis have a competitive advantage. By leveraging the power of data analysis, businesses can stay ahead of the competition, adapt to changing market conditions, and drive innovation.

Chapter 25: The 28 Struggles Everyone Faces and How to Conquer Them

Struggles are a natural part of life. From the moment we are born, we are faced with challenges and obstacles that we must overcome. Whether it's learning to walk, ride a bike, or excel in school, struggles are an inevitable part of the human experience. However, it is through these struggles that we have the opportunity for personal growth and development.

No one is exempt from facing struggles. From the richest to the poorest, the most successful to the least successful, everyone faces their own unique set of challenges. It is how we choose to respond to these struggles that determines our character and shapes our future. Overcoming struggles requires resilience, determination, and a willingness to learn from our mistakes.

Struggle #1: Procrastination and How to Overcome It

Procrastination is a common struggle that many people face. It is the act of delaying or postponing tasks that need to be completed. There are several causes of procrastination, including fear of failure, lack of motivation, and poor time management.

To overcome procrastination, it is important to identify the root cause of your procrastination. Are you afraid of failing? Are you lacking motivation? Once you have identified the cause, you can then take steps to address it. For example, if you are afraid of failing, you can work on building your confidence and overcoming your fear of failure.

In addition to addressing the root cause of your procrastination, there are several tips that can help you overcome this struggle. One tip is to break tasks down into smaller, more manageable chunks. This can make tasks feel less overwhelming and more achievable. Another tip is to create a schedule or to-do list and stick to it. This can help you stay organized and focused on completing tasks in a timely manner.

Struggle #2: Fear of Failure and How to Build Confidence

Fear of failure is another common struggle that many people face. It is the fear of not meeting expectations or falling short of goals. This fear can be paralyzing and prevent individuals from taking risks or pursuing their dreams.

There are several causes of fear of failure, including past experiences of failure, perfectionism, and negative self-talk. To build confidence and overcome this fear, it is important to address these underlying causes.

One tip for building confidence is to focus on your strengths and accomplishments. Take time to reflect on your past successes and remind yourself of your abilities. Another tip is to set realistic goals and break them down into smaller, more achievable steps. This can help build confidence as you see yourself making progress towards your goals.

It is also important to challenge negative self-talk and replace it with positive affirmations. Instead of telling yourself that you will fail, remind yourself that you are capable and deserving of success. Surrounding yourself with supportive and positive people can also help boost your confidence and provide encouragement.

Struggle #3: Time Management and How to Prioritize Tasks

Poor time management is a struggle that many people face. It is the inability to effectively manage and prioritize tasks, resulting in a feeling of being overwhelmed and stressed.

There are several causes of poor time management, including procrastination, lack of organization, and difficulty prioritizing tasks. To improve time management skills, it is important to address these underlying causes.

One tip for improving time management is to create a schedule or to-do list. This can help you visualize your tasks and prioritize them based on importance and urgency. Another tip is to eliminate distractions, such as turning off notifications on your phone or finding a quiet workspace.

It can also be helpful to break tasks down into smaller, more manageable chunks. This can make tasks feel less overwhelming and more achievable. Additionally, it is important to set realistic expectations for yourself and avoid overcommitting. Learning to say no and delegate tasks when necessary can help free up time and reduce stress.

Struggle #4: Lack of Motivation and How to Stay Inspired

Lack of motivation is a struggle that many people face at some point in their lives. It is the feeling of not having the drive or enthusiasm to pursue goals or complete tasks.

There are several causes of lack of motivation, including fear of failure, burnout, and lack of clarity or purpose. To stay inspired and motivated, it is important to address these underlying causes.

One tip for staying inspired is to set clear goals and create a vision board or visual representation of your goals. This can help you stay focused and motivated as you work towards achieving them. Another tip is to find your passion and pursue activities or hobbies that bring you joy and fulfillment.

It can also be helpful to surround yourself with positive and supportive people who inspire and motivate you. Additionally, taking care of your physical and mental well-being through exercise, proper nutrition, and self-care can help boost your energy levels and increase motivation.

Struggle #5: Negative Self-Talk and How to Cultivate a Positive Mindset

Negative self-talk is a struggle that many people face. It is the habit of criticizing oneself or engaging in negative thoughts and beliefs about oneself.

There are several causes of negative self-talk, including past experiences of failure or criticism, low self-esteem, and comparison to others. To cultivate a positive mindset and overcome negative self-talk, it is important to address these underlying causes.

One tip for cultivating a positive mindset is to practice self-compassion. Treat yourself with kindness and understanding, just as you would treat a friend or loved one. Another tip is to challenge negative thoughts and replace them with positive affirmations. For example, if you catch yourself thinking "I'm not good enough," replace it with "I am capable and deserving of success."

It can also be helpful to surround yourself with positive influences, such as uplifting books, podcasts, or motivational speakers. Additionally, practicing gratitude and focusing on the positive aspects of your life can help shift your mindset from negative to positive.

Struggle #6: Perfectionism and How to Embrace Imperfection

Perfectionism is a struggle that many people face. It is the tendency to set unrealistically high standards for oneself and strive for flawlessness.

There are several causes of perfectionism, including fear of failure, fear of judgment, and a desire for control. To embrace imperfection and overcome perfectionism, it is important to address these underlying causes.

One tip for embracing imperfection is to set realistic expectations for yourself. Understand that no one is perfect and that making mistakes is a natural part of the learning process. Another tip is to practice self-compassion and remind yourself that you are human and deserving of love and acceptance.

It can also be helpful to challenge perfectionistic thoughts and replace them with more realistic and compassionate ones. For example, if you catch yourself thinking "I have to be perfect," replace it with "I am doing my best and that is enough."

Additionally, it can be beneficial to seek support from others who have overcome perfectionism or who can provide guidance and encouragement. Surrounding yourself with people who value effort and progress over perfection can help shift your mindset and embrace imperfection.

Struggle #7: Overthinking and How to Practice Mindfulness

Overthinking is a struggle that many people face. It is the habit of dwelling on past events or worrying about future outcomes, often leading to feelings of anxiety or stress.

There are several causes of overthinking, including fear of failure, lack of control, and a desire for certainty. To practice mindfulness and overcome overthinking, it is important to address these underlying causes.

One tip for practicing mindfulness is to focus on the present moment. Engage in activities that bring you joy and fully immerse yourself in the experience. Another tip is to practice deep breathing or meditation to help calm the mind and reduce anxiety.

It can also be helpful to challenge negative or anxious thoughts and replace them with more positive and realistic ones. For example, if you catch yourself worrying about the future, remind yourself that you cannot predict or control everything and that it is okay to let go of the need for certainty.

Additionally, it can be beneficial to create a routine or schedule that includes time for relaxation and self-care. Taking breaks and engaging in activities that promote relaxation, such as reading, taking a walk, or practicing yoga, can help reduce overthinking and promote a sense of calm.

Struggle #8: Imposter Syndrome and How to Recognize Your Worth

Imposter syndrome is a struggle that many people face. It is the feeling of not deserving success or accomplishments and fearing being exposed as a fraud.

There are several causes of imposter syndrome, including fear of failure, perfectionism, and comparison to others. To recognize your worth and overcome imposter syndrome, it is important to address these underlying causes.

One tip for recognizing your worth is to celebrate your accomplishments and acknowledge your strengths. Take time to reflect on your achievements and remind yourself of the hard work and effort you have put in. Another tip is to challenge self-doubt and replace it with self-compassion and positive affirmations.

It can also be helpful to surround yourself with supportive and encouraging people who believe in your abilities. Seek out mentors or role models who can provide guidance and support as you navigate through imposter syndrome.

Additionally, it can be beneficial to practice self-care and prioritize your well-being. Taking care of your physical and mental health can help boost your confidence and remind you of your worth.

Struggle #9: Burnout and How to Practice Self-Care

Burnout is a struggle that many people face, especially in today's fast-paced and demanding world. It is the feeling of being physically, mentally, and emotionally exhausted due to prolonged stress or overwork.

There are several causes of burnout, including excessive workload, lack of work-life balance, and neglecting self-care. To practice self-care and avoid burnout, it is important to address these underlying causes.

One tip for practicing self-care is to set boundaries and prioritize your well-being. Learn to say no to excessive demands or commitments that may lead to burnout. Another tip is to schedule regular breaks and engage in activities that promote relaxation and rejuvenation.

It can also be helpful to practice stress management techniques, such as deep breathing, meditation, or exercise. These activities can help reduce stress levels and promote a sense of calm.

Additionally, it is important to take care of your physical health through proper nutrition, exercise, and adequate sleep. Taking care of your body can help increase energy levels and reduce the risk of burnout.

Overcoming Struggles is a Journey, Not a Destination.

Overcoming struggles is not an easy task. It takes time, effort, and a willingness to learn from our mistakes. It is important to be patient and kind to ourselves as we navigate through life's challenges.

Remember that personal growth and development is a lifelong journey. Each struggle we face provides an opportunity for growth and learning. By addressing the underlying causes of our struggles and implementing strategies for overcoming them, we can become stronger, more resilient individuals.

So the next time you find yourself facing a struggle, remember that you are not alone. Everyone faces challenges and obstacles in life. Embrace the journey of overcoming struggles and trust in your ability to grow and thrive.

Chapter 26: The Surprising Benefits of Accepting Others for Who They Are

Acceptance is a fundamental aspect of human interaction and plays a crucial role in our overall well-being. It is the ability to acknowledge and embrace the reality of a situation or another person without judgment or resistance. Acceptance allows us to let go of control and expectations, and instead, focus on understanding and compassion. In our fast-paced and often judgmental society, acceptance has become increasingly important for fostering healthy relationships, improving mental health, and promoting personal growth.

Acceptance vs. Tolerance: Understanding the Difference

While acceptance and tolerance are often used interchangeably, they have distinct meanings. Tolerance refers to the ability to endure or tolerate something that one may not agree with or find acceptable. It implies a level of discomfort or disagreement but still allows for coexistence. On the other hand, acceptance goes beyond mere tolerance. It involves embracing and acknowledging the differences or realities of others without judgment or resistance.

Acceptance requires an open mind and a willingness to understand and empathize with others' perspectives. It is about recognizing that everyone has their own unique experiences, beliefs, and values, and that these differences should be respected rather than judged.

Improved Relationships: How Acceptance Can Strengthen Connections

Acceptance plays a vital role in improving relationships by fostering understanding, trust, and empathy. When we accept others for who they are, we create a safe space for them to express themselves authentically. This allows for open communication and deeper connections.

For example, in a romantic relationship, acceptance means embracing your partner's flaws and imperfections rather than trying to change them. It means understanding that no one is perfect and that it is through acceptance that we can truly love someone unconditionally.

In friendships, acceptance allows us to appreciate our friends' unique qualities and support them without judgment. It creates an environment where individuals feel comfortable being themselves, leading to stronger and more fulfilling relationships.

Increased Empathy: The Power of Seeing Things from Another's Perspective

Empathy is the ability to understand and share the feelings of another person. It is closely linked to acceptance, as accepting others' experiences and perspectives is essential for developing empathy.

When we practice acceptance, we open ourselves up to seeing things from another's perspective. We let go of our preconceived notions and biases and truly listen to others' stories and experiences. This not only deepens our understanding of others but also allows us to connect with them on a deeper level.

By cultivating empathy through acceptance, we become more compassionate and understanding individuals. We are better able to support others in their struggles and celebrate their successes, leading to more meaningful relationships and a more harmonious society.

Boosted Self-Esteem: How Accepting Others Can Improve Our Own Self-Image

Acceptance is not only important for our relationships with others but also for our relationship with ourselves. When we accept others for who they are, we also learn to accept ourselves.

Accepting others' differences and imperfections helps us realize that we too are imperfect and that it is okay. It allows us to let go of unrealistic expectations and self-judgment, leading to improved self-esteem.

When we accept ourselves, flaws and all, we become more confident in our abilities and more comfortable in our own skin. We no longer feel the need to compare ourselves to others or seek validation from external sources. Instead, we can focus on personal growth and self-improvement without the burden of self-criticism.

Reduced Stress: The Benefits of Letting Go of Judgment and Criticism

Judgment and criticism are sources of stress that can negatively impact our mental and emotional well-being. When we judge or criticize others, we create a negative energy that not only affects them but also affects us.

By practicing acceptance, we let go of the need to judge or criticize others. We recognize that everyone is on their own unique journey and that it is not our place to pass judgment. This release of judgment and criticism allows us to experience a sense of peace and reduces the stress and negativity in our lives.

Acceptance also helps us let go of the need for control. When we accept that we cannot control everything or change others, we free ourselves from the burden of trying to fix or change things beyond our control. This acceptance leads to a greater sense of peace and contentment.

Improved Mental Health: Acceptance as a Tool for Managing Anxiety and Depression

Acceptance plays a crucial role in managing anxiety and depression. When we resist or deny our emotions or circumstances, we create internal conflict and distress. Acceptance allows us to acknowledge and embrace our emotions and experiences without judgment or resistance.

By accepting our emotions, we can process them in a healthy way and work towards finding solutions or seeking support when needed. Acceptance also helps us let go of the need for perfection or control, reducing feelings of anxiety and overwhelm.

In addition, acceptance can help us navigate challenging life circumstances. When faced with adversity, accepting the reality of the situation allows us to focus on finding solutions rather than dwelling on what could have been or what should be.

Increased Creativity: How Embracing Differences Can Spark Innovation

Acceptance is not only important for personal relationships but also for fostering creativity and innovation. When we embrace differences and accept diverse perspectives, we create an environment that encourages new ideas and approaches.

By accepting that there is no one right way of doing things, we open ourselves up to new possibilities and alternative solutions. This mindset shift sparks creativity and allows for innovative thinking.

In a team setting, acceptance of diverse perspectives fosters collaboration and encourages individuals to contribute their unique skills and ideas. This diversity of thought leads to more creative problem-solving and ultimately, better outcomes.

Enhanced Diversity: The Importance of Celebrating and Embracing Different Cultures

Acceptance is essential for promoting diversity and inclusion in society. When we accept and celebrate different cultures, we create a more inclusive and harmonious world.

By embracing different cultures, we gain a broader perspective and appreciation for the richness and diversity of human experiences. This acceptance allows us to learn from one another, break down stereotypes, and build bridges between communities.

Acceptance of different cultures also promotes equality and social justice. It challenges discriminatory practices and encourages individuals to stand up against injustice.

Improved Communication: How Acceptance Can Improve Our Ability to Connect with Others

Effective communication is built on a foundation of acceptance. When we accept others for who they are, we create an environment where open and honest communication can thrive.

Acceptance allows us to listen without judgment, truly hear what others are saying, and respond with empathy and understanding. It fosters trust and creates a safe space for individuals to express themselves authentically.

By practicing acceptance in our communication, we can resolve conflicts more effectively, build stronger relationships, and foster a sense of belonging and connection.

The Transformative Power of Acceptance in Our Lives

In conclusion, acceptance is a transformative force that has the power to improve our relationships, enhance our mental health, boost our self-esteem, spark creativity, promote diversity, and improve our ability to connect with others.

By practicing acceptance in our daily lives, we can create a more compassionate and inclusive society. It starts with accepting ourselves and then extending that acceptance to others. Through acceptance, we can build stronger relationships, foster empathy, reduce stress, manage anxiety and depression, embrace diversity, enhance creativity, and improve our communication skills.

Let us embrace the power of acceptance and create a world where everyone feels seen, heard, and valued for who they are.

Chapter 27: The Art of Self-Empowerment: How to Take Control of Your Life

Self-empowerment is the process of taking control of one's life, making positive changes, and becoming the best version of oneself. It involves recognizing and overcoming limiting beliefs, setting goals, taking risks, building resilience, practicing self-care, developing a growth mindset, finding passion and purpose, cultivating a support system, and celebrating successes. Self-empowerment is important because it allows individuals to live a fulfilling and meaningful life, achieve their goals, and overcome obstacles.

Understanding Limiting Beliefs

Limiting beliefs are negative thoughts or beliefs that hold us back from reaching our full potential. They are often deeply ingrained and can stem from past experiences, societal conditioning, or fear of failure. Examples of common limiting beliefs include "I'm not good enough," "I don't deserve success," or "I'll never be able to achieve my dreams." These beliefs can be identified by paying attention to negative self-talk or patterns of self-sabotage.

To overcome limiting beliefs, it is important to challenge them and replace them with positive affirmations. This involves questioning the validity of the belief and gathering evidence to prove it wrong. For example, if the belief is "I'm not good enough," one can challenge it by listing past accomplishments or positive qualities. It is also helpful to surround oneself with positive influences and seek support from others who believe in our abilities.

The Power of Positive Affirmations and Self-Talk

Positive affirmations are statements that are repeated to oneself in order to challenge negative thoughts and beliefs. They can help improve self-esteem and confidence by reprogramming the subconscious mind with positive messages. Examples of positive affirmations include "I am capable of achieving my goals," "I deserve success," or "I am worthy of love and happiness."

Incorporating positive affirmations into daily life can be done through various methods such as writing them down, saying them out loud, or creating visual reminders. It is important to choose affirmations that resonate with oneself and to repeat them consistently. Additionally, practicing positive self-talk throughout the day can help reinforce positive beliefs and counteract negative thoughts.

Setting Goals and Creating a Plan of Action

Setting goals is an important part of self-empowerment as it provides direction and motivation. Goals can be short-term or long-term and can encompass various areas of life such as career, relationships, health, or personal development. It is important to set goals that are specific, measurable, achievable, relevant, and time-bound (SMART).

Once goals are set, creating a plan of action is essential to achieve them. This involves breaking down the goals into smaller tasks or milestones and creating a timeline for completion. It is also helpful to identify potential obstacles or challenges and come up with strategies to overcome them. Staying motivated and accountable can be achieved by tracking progress, celebrating small wins, and seeking support from others.

Overcoming Fear and Taking Risks

Fear is a natural human emotion that often holds us back from taking risks or pursuing our dreams. It can manifest as fear of failure, fear of rejection, or fear of the unknown. However, overcoming fear is crucial for self-empowerment as it allows us to step outside our comfort zone and grow.

To overcome fear, it is important to acknowledge and understand it. This can be done by identifying the specific fears and questioning their validity. It is also helpful to reframe fear as an opportunity for growth and learning. Taking small steps towards facing fears can gradually build confidence and reduce anxiety. Embracing failure as a learning opportunity can also help overcome fear by shifting the focus from avoiding failure to embracing growth.

Building Resilience and Bouncing Back from Setbacks

Resilience is the ability to bounce back from setbacks or adversity. It involves developing a strong mindset, adapting to change, and maintaining a positive outlook. Building resilience is an important aspect of self-empowerment as it allows individuals to overcome obstacles and continue moving forward.

To build resilience, it is important to cultivate a positive mindset and practice self-compassion. This involves reframing negative thoughts or situations into positive ones and focusing on strengths and solutions. It is also helpful to develop healthy coping mechanisms such as practicing mindfulness, seeking support from others, or engaging in activities that bring joy and relaxation.

Bouncing back from setbacks and adversity can be achieved by learning from the experience, finding meaning or purpose in the situation, and setting new goals. It is important to remember that setbacks are a natural part of life and can provide valuable lessons and opportunities for growth.

The Role of Self-Care in Self-Empowerment

Self-care is the practice of taking care of one's physical, mental, and emotional well-being. It is an essential aspect of self-empowerment as it allows individuals to recharge, reduce stress, and maintain a healthy balance in life. Self-care involves activities that bring joy, relaxation, and fulfillment.

Importance of self-care for mental and physical health

Self-care is important for mental and physical health as it helps reduce stress, prevent burnout, and improve overall well-being. Taking time for oneself allows individuals to recharge and replenish their energy levels. It also helps improve focus, productivity, and creativity.

How self-care can improve self-empowerment

Self-care plays a crucial role in self-empowerment as it allows individuals to prioritize their needs and set boundaries. By taking care of oneself, individuals can develop a stronger sense of self-worth and confidence. Self-care also provides an opportunity for self-reflection and personal growth.

Tips for incorporating self-care into daily life

Incorporating self-care into daily life can be done through various activities such as exercise, meditation, journaling, spending time in nature, or engaging in hobbies. It is important to prioritize self-care and make it a non-negotiable part of daily routine. Setting boundaries and saying no to activities or commitments that drain energy is also important for self-care.

Developing a Growth Mindset and Embracing Change

A growth mindset is the belief that abilities and intelligence can be developed through effort, practice, and learning. It is the opposite of a fixed mindset, which believes that abilities are fixed and cannot be changed. Developing a growth mindset is crucial for self-empowerment as it allows individuals to embrace challenges, learn from failures, and adapt to change.

To develop a growth mindset, it is important to embrace challenges and view them as opportunities for growth. This involves reframing failures as learning experiences and focusing on the process rather than the outcome. It is also helpful to seek feedback from others and be open to new ideas or perspectives.

Embracing change can be achieved by being flexible and adaptable. It is important to let go of the need for control and embrace uncertainty. Taking small steps towards change can gradually build confidence and reduce resistance. It is also helpful to surround oneself with positive influences and seek support from others who have successfully navigated change.

Finding Your Passion and Purpose in Life

Finding passion and purpose in life is an important aspect of self-empowerment as it provides meaning and fulfillment. Passion is the intense enthusiasm or interest in something, while purpose is the reason for one's existence or the impact one wants to make in the world.

To discover passions and purpose, it is important to explore different interests, reflect on values and strengths, and listen to intuition. This can be done through activities such as journaling, brainstorming, or seeking new experiences. It is also helpful to seek inspiration from others who have found their passions and purpose.

Pursuing passions and purpose involves setting goals and taking action. It is important to align actions with values and to stay committed and focused. It is also helpful to seek support from others who share similar passions or goals.

Cultivating a Support System and Seeking Guidance

Having a support system is crucial for self-empowerment as it provides encouragement, accountability, and guidance. A support system can consist of friends, family, mentors, or like-minded individuals who believe in one's abilities and provide support.

To cultivate a support system, it is important to surround oneself with positive influences and seek out individuals who share similar goals or values. This can be done through joining communities or groups that align with one's interests or passions. It is also helpful to seek guidance from mentors or coaches who have successfully achieved similar goals.

Seeking guidance and mentorship can provide valuable insights, advice, and accountability. It is important to be open to feedback and to actively seek out opportunities for growth and learning. Building relationships with mentors or coaches can provide ongoing support and guidance throughout the self-empowerment journey.

Celebrating Your Successes and Maintaining Momentum

Celebrating successes is an important part of self-empowerment as it provides motivation, boosts confidence, and reinforces positive behaviors. Celebrating small wins along the way can help maintain momentum and inspire continued growth.

Importance of celebrating successes

Celebrating successes is important as it acknowledges progress and achievements. It provides a sense of accomplishment and boosts self-esteem. Celebrating successes also helps maintain motivation and inspires continued effort.

How to maintain momentum and continue self-empowerment

Maintaining momentum involves setting new goals, staying focused, and continuing to take action. It is important to reflect on past successes and use them as motivation for future endeavors. Staying connected with a support system can also provide ongoing encouragement and accountability.

Tips for staying motivated and inspired

Staying motivated and inspired can be achieved by setting meaningful goals, visualizing success, and practicing gratitude. It is important to stay focused on the bigger picture and remind oneself of the reasons for pursuing self-empowerment. Engaging in activities that bring joy and fulfillment can also help maintain motivation and inspiration.

Self-empowerment is a journey of personal growth and transformation. It involves recognizing and overcoming limiting beliefs, setting goals, taking risks, building resilience, practicing self-care, developing a growth mindset, finding passion and purpose, cultivating a support system, and celebrating successes. By embracing self-empowerment, individuals can live a fulfilling and meaningful life, achieve their goals, and overcome obstacles. It is never too late to start the journey of self-empowerment and create positive change in one's life.

Chapter 28: The Power of Active Listening: How to Build Stronger Relationships

Active listening is a crucial skill that plays a significant role in effective communication. It involves fully engaging with the speaker, paying attention to both verbal and non-verbal cues, and demonstrating understanding and empathy. Active listening goes beyond simply hearing the words being spoken; it requires a genuine effort to comprehend the message and respond appropriately. By actively listening, we can build stronger relationships, enhance problem-solving abilities, and strengthen connections with others.

Active listening is the process of fully focusing on and comprehending what someone is saying. It involves giving our undivided attention to the speaker, both verbally and non-verbally. This means avoiding distractions, maintaining eye contact, nodding or using other non-verbal cues to show understanding, and providing feedback when necessary. Active listening is not just about hearing the words being spoken; it is about understanding the underlying message and responding in a way that shows empathy and respect.

The benefits of active listening are numerous. Firstly, it improves understanding and empathy. By actively listening to someone, we can gain a deeper understanding of their thoughts, feelings, and perspectives. This allows us to connect with them on a more meaningful level and respond in a way that shows empathy and support. Active listening also increases trust and respect in relationships. When we actively listen to someone, they feel heard and valued, which strengthens the bond between us. Additionally, active listening enhances problem-solving and decision-making abilities. By fully understanding someone's concerns or needs, we can work together to find solutions or make informed decisions. Overall, active listening helps build stronger relationships, fosters effective communication, and promotes mutual understanding.

The Benefits of Active Listening in Building Stronger Relationships

Active listening plays a crucial role in building stronger relationships by improving understanding and empathy, increasing trust and respect, enhancing problem-solving and decision-making abilities, and strengthening connections and bonds.

One of the key benefits of active listening is improved understanding and empathy. When we actively listen to someone, we make a conscious effort to comprehend their message and perspective. This allows us to gain a deeper understanding of their thoughts, feelings, and experiences. By truly understanding where someone is coming from, we can respond in a way that shows empathy and support. This helps build trust and strengthens the relationship.

Active listening also increases trust and respect in relationships. When we actively listen to someone, they feel heard and valued. This creates a sense of trust and respect between both parties. By demonstrating that we are fully present and engaged in the conversation, we show that we value the other person's thoughts and opinions. This fosters a stronger bond and encourages open and honest communication.

Furthermore, active listening enhances problem-solving and decision-making abilities. By actively listening to someone's concerns or needs, we can work together to find solutions or make informed decisions. Active listening allows us to gather all the necessary information and understand the underlying issues before offering suggestions or making decisions. This collaborative approach leads to more effective problem-solving and decision-making processes.

Lastly, active listening strengthens connections and bonds between individuals. When we actively listen to someone, we create a space for open and honest communication. This fosters a sense of connection and understanding between both parties. Active listening helps build rapport and encourages individuals to share their thoughts, feelings, and experiences more freely. This strengthens the bond between individuals and promotes a deeper level of connection.

The Difference between Active Listening and Passive Listening

Passive listening is the opposite of active listening. It involves simply hearing the words being spoken without fully engaging with the speaker or comprehending the message. Passive listeners may be physically present but mentally absent, allowing their minds to wander or focusing on other things instead of actively listening.

The key difference between active listening and passive listening lies in the level of engagement and comprehension. Active listening requires full engagement with the speaker, both verbally and non-verbally. It involves paying attention to both the words being spoken and the non-verbal cues, such as body language and tone of voice. Active listeners make a conscious effort to understand the underlying message and respond appropriately.

On the other hand, passive listening lacks engagement and comprehension. Passive listeners may hear the words being spoken but fail to fully understand or respond to the message. They may be distracted, preoccupied with their own thoughts, or simply not interested in what the speaker has to say. Passive listening can lead to misunderstandings, miscommunication, and a lack of connection between individuals.

Active listening is more effective than passive listening for several reasons. Firstly, active listening allows for better understanding and comprehension of the message. By actively engaging with the speaker and paying attention to both verbal and non-verbal cues, active listeners can gain a deeper understanding of the underlying message. This leads to more effective communication and reduces the chances of misunderstandings.

Secondly, active listening shows respect and empathy towards the speaker. When we actively listen to someone, we demonstrate that we value their thoughts and opinions. This creates a sense of trust and respect in the relationship. Passive listening, on the other hand, can make the speaker feel ignored or unimportant.

Lastly, active listening promotes a deeper level of connection between individuals. By actively engaging with the speaker and demonstrating understanding and empathy, active listeners create a safe space for open and honest communication. This fosters a stronger bond and encourages individuals to share their thoughts, feelings, and experiences more freely.

How to Practice Active Listening: Tips and Techniques

Practicing active listening involves several key techniques that can help improve our ability to fully engage with others, comprehend their message, and respond appropriately.

The first tip for practicing active listening is to pay attention and stay focused. This means avoiding distractions and giving our undivided attention to the speaker. We can do this by putting away our phones, turning off the TV or radio, and finding a quiet and comfortable space for the conversation. By eliminating distractions, we can fully engage with the speaker and show that we value their thoughts and opinions.

Another technique for active listening is asking open-ended questions. Open-ended questions encourage the speaker to provide more detailed and thoughtful responses, allowing us to gain a deeper understanding of their perspective. By asking questions such as "Can you tell me more about that?" or "How did that make you feel?", we can encourage the speaker to share more information and provide us with a clearer picture of their thoughts and experiences.

Paraphrasing and summarizing are also important techniques for active listening. Paraphrasing involves restating the speaker's message in our own words to ensure that we have understood it correctly. This allows the speaker to confirm or clarify their message if necessary. Summarizing involves providing a concise overview of the main points discussed during the conversation. This helps both parties stay on track and ensures that all important information has been addressed.

Lastly, providing feedback and validation is crucial for active listening. Feedback can involve nodding, using appropriate facial expressions, or providing verbal cues such as "I understand" or "That makes sense." Validation involves acknowledging the speaker's feelings and experiences, even if we may not agree with them. By providing feedback and validation, we show that we are actively engaged in the conversation and value the speaker's thoughts and opinions.

The Role of Empathy in Active Listening

Empathy plays a vital role in active listening. It involves understanding and sharing the feelings, thoughts, and experiences of another person. By cultivating empathy in our communication, we can better connect with others, demonstrate understanding and support, and build stronger relationships.

Empathy is the ability to understand and share the feelings, thoughts, and experiences of another person. It goes beyond sympathy, which involves feeling sorry for someone's situation. Empathy requires putting ourselves in the other person's shoes and truly understanding their perspective.

Empathy is crucial in active listening because it allows us to connect with others on a deeper level. By understanding and sharing their feelings, thoughts, and experiences, we can demonstrate genuine support and understanding. This creates a safe space for open and honest communication and strengthens the bond between individuals.

Cultivating empathy in communication involves several key practices. Firstly, it requires active listening, as discussed earlier. By fully engaging with the speaker and comprehending their message, we can better understand their perspective and respond in a way that shows empathy.

Secondly, empathy involves suspending judgment and biases. It requires setting aside our own preconceived notions or beliefs and truly listening to the other person's perspective. This allows us to see things from their point of view and respond in a way that shows empathy and understanding.

Lastly, empathy requires practicing compassion. Compassion involves showing kindness, understanding, and support towards others. By demonstrating compassion in our communication, we can create a safe and supportive environment for open and honest dialogue.

Overcoming Common Barriers to Active Listening

There are several common barriers that can hinder our ability to practice active listening effectively. These barriers include distractions and interruptions, prejudices and biases, lack of interest or motivation, among others. However, there are strategies that can help overcome these barriers and improve our active listening skills.

Distractions and interruptions are common barriers to active listening. In today's fast-paced world, it is easy to get distracted by notifications on our phones or other external stimuli. To overcome this barrier, it is important to eliminate distractions by turning off notifications or finding a quiet space for the conversation. Additionally, setting aside dedicated time for active listening can help ensure that we are fully present and engaged in the conversation.

Prejudices and biases can also hinder our ability to practice active listening. These biases can cloud our judgment and prevent us from truly understanding the other person's perspective. To overcome this barrier, it is important to be aware of our own biases and actively challenge them. This can be done by seeking out diverse perspectives, engaging in open-minded discussions, and practicing empathy.

Lack of interest or motivation is another barrier to active listening. If we are not genuinely interested in what the other person has to say, it can be challenging to fully engage with them and comprehend their message. To overcome this barrier, it is important to find ways to cultivate curiosity and genuine interest in others. This can be done by asking open-ended questions, seeking out new perspectives, and actively seeking to learn from others.

Overall, overcoming these barriers requires a conscious effort to be fully present and engaged in the conversation. By eliminating distractions, challenging biases, and cultivating genuine interest, we can improve our active listening skills and build stronger relationships.

The Importance of Non-Verbal Communication in Active Listening

Non-verbal communication plays a crucial role in active listening. It involves the use of body language, facial expressions, gestures, and tone of voice to convey messages and emotions. By interpreting and responding to non-verbal cues, we can better understand the speaker's message and demonstrate empathy and support.

Non-verbal communication refers to the use of body language, facial expressions, gestures, and tone of voice to convey messages and emotions. It is an essential component of effective communication as it provides additional context and meaning to the words being spoken.

Examples of non-verbal cues include maintaining eye contact, nodding or using other facial expressions to show understanding or agreement, using appropriate hand gestures to emphasize points or convey emotions, and using tone of voice to convey emotions such as excitement or concern.

Interpreting non-verbal cues is an important part of active listening. By paying attention to the speaker's body language, facial expressions, and tone of voice, we can gain a deeper understanding of their emotions and intentions. This allows us to respond in a way that shows empathy and support.

Responding to non-verbal cues is equally important. By using appropriate body language, facial expressions, and tone of voice, we can convey our understanding and support to the speaker. This helps create a safe space for open and honest communication and strengthens the bond between individuals.

Active Listening in Professional Settings: Building Stronger Teams and Partnerships

Active listening is particularly important in professional settings as it can help build stronger teams and partnerships. By actively listening to colleagues, clients, or business partners, we can foster effective communication, improve teamwork and collaboration, and enhance professional relationships.

Active listening is crucial in the workplace as it promotes effective communication. By actively listening to colleagues or clients, we can better understand their needs, concerns, or ideas. This allows us to respond in a way that shows empathy and support, leading to more productive and efficient communication.

Active listening also improves teamwork and collaboration. By actively engaging with team members and comprehending their perspectives, we can work together more effectively towards common goals. Active listening allows us to gather all the necessary information, understand different viewpoints, and find common ground. This fosters a sense of collaboration and strengthens the team dynamic.

Furthermore, active listening enhances professional relationships. By actively listening to colleagues or business partners, we demonstrate that we value their thoughts and opinions. This creates a sense of trust and respect in the relationship. Active listening helps build rapport and encourages open and honest communication, leading to stronger professional relationships.

Active Listening in Personal Relationships: Strengthening Bonds with Family and Friends

Active listening is equally important in personal relationships as it can help strengthen bonds with family and friends. By actively listening to loved ones, we can improve communication and understanding, demonstrate empathy and support, and foster deeper connections.

Active listening is crucial in personal relationships as it improves communication and understanding. By actively listening to loved ones, we can better understand their thoughts, feelings, and experiences. This allows us to respond in a way that shows empathy and support, leading to more meaningful and fulfilling conversations.

Active listening also demonstrates empathy and support in personal relationships. By actively engaging with loved ones and comprehending their perspectives, we can show that we value their thoughts and opinions. This creates a safe space for open and honest communication and strengthens the bond between individuals.

Furthermore, active listening fosters deeper connections with family and friends. By actively listening to loved ones, we create a space for them to share their thoughts, feelings, and experiences more freely. This strengthens the bond between individuals and promotes a deeper level of connection.

Active Listening in Conflict Resolution: Finding Common Ground and Resolving Disputes

Active listening is particularly important in conflict resolution as it can help find common ground and resolve disputes. By actively listening to all parties involved, we can better understand their perspectives, demonstrate empathy and understanding, and work towards finding mutually beneficial solutions.

Active listening is crucial in conflict resolution as it allows us to gain a deeper understanding of all perspectives involved. By actively engaging with each party and comprehending their viewpoints, we can better understand the underlying issues and concerns. This allows us to respond in a way that shows empathy and support, leading to more effective conflict resolution.

Active listening also helps find common ground in conflicts. By actively listening to all parties involved , individuals can better understand each other's perspectives and concerns. This understanding can lead to the identification of shared interests or goals, which can serve as a foundation for resolving conflicts. Active listening allows for the exploration of different viewpoints and encourages open and honest communication, fostering an environment where compromise and collaboration are more likely to occur. Additionally, active listening helps to build trust and rapport among those involved in the conflict, creating a more positive and constructive atmosphere for finding common ground.

Chapter 29: Creating Effective Social Stories: Tips and Tricks for Parents and Educators

Social stories are a powerful tool used to help individuals with autism navigate social situations and understand appropriate behaviors. They provide a structured and visual way to teach social skills and promote understanding of social expectations. In this blog post, we will explore the importance of social stories for individuals with autism and provide a step-by-step guide on how to create effective social stories. We will also discuss tips for writing clear and concise stories, using visuals to enhance the stories, incorporating personalization, addressing challenging behaviors, using social stories in different settings, evaluating their effectiveness, and collaborating with professionals for successful implementation.

What are Social Stories and Why are They Important?

Social stories are short narratives that describe a specific social situation or behavior in a clear and concise manner. They are typically written from the perspective of the individual with autism and use simple language and visuals to convey information. Social stories are important for individuals with autism because they provide a structured way to teach social skills and promote understanding of social expectations. They help individuals with autism navigate social situations that may be confusing or overwhelming, and provide them with strategies for appropriate behavior.

Understanding the Purpose of Social Stories for Children with Autism

Children with autism have unique needs when it comes to social interactions. They may struggle with understanding nonverbal cues, interpreting social situations, and knowing how to respond appropriately. Social stories address these needs by providing clear and concrete information about social expectations and behaviors. For example, a social story may explain how to greet someone, take turns in a conversation, or handle frustration. By providing this information in a structured and visual format, social stories help children with autism understand what is expected of them in different social situations.

Social stories can be helpful in a variety of situations. For example, they can be used to prepare a child for a new experience or event, such as going to the dentist or starting school. They can also be used to teach specific social skills, such as sharing or taking turns. Additionally, social stories can be used to address challenging behaviors, such as hitting or biting. By providing clear and concrete information about appropriate behavior, social stories help children with autism understand what is expected of them and provide them with strategies for success.

The Components of Effective Social Stories

Effective social stories have several key components that contribute to their effectiveness. These components include:

1. Clear and concise language: Social stories should use simple and straightforward language that is easy for the individual with autism to understand. Avoid using complex or abstract language, and focus on providing concrete information.

2. Visual supports: Visual supports, such as pictures or symbols, can enhance the understanding of social stories for individuals with autism. They provide a visual representation of the information being conveyed

and can help individuals with autism make connections between the story and real-life situations.

3. Personalization: Social stories should be personalized to the individual with autism to make them more relatable and meaningful. Use the individual's name and include specific details that are relevant to their experiences.

4. Positive tone: Social stories should have a positive tone and focus on desired behaviors rather than negative behaviors. They should highlight the benefits of appropriate behavior and provide strategies for success.

How to Create a Social Story: Step-by-Step Guide

Creating a social story involves several steps. Here is a step-by-step guide to help you create an effective social story:

1. Identify the target behavior or situation: Determine the specific behavior or situation that you want to address in the social story. For example, if you want to teach a child how to greet someone, the target behavior would be greeting someone.

2. Gather information: Gather information about the target behavior or situation. This may involve observing the behavior or talking to others who are familiar with the situation.

3. Write the story: Write the social story using clear and concise language. Use simple sentences and focus on providing concrete information. Include visuals to enhance understanding.

4. Review and revise: Review the social story for accuracy and clarity. Make any necessary revisions to ensure that the story effectively conveys the desired information.

5. Share the story: Share the social story with the individual with autism. Read it together and discuss the information presented. Encourage questions and provide additional support as needed.

Tips for Writing Clear and Concise Social Stories

Clear and concise language is important in social stories to ensure that the information is easily understood by individuals with autism. Here are some tips for writing in a clear and concise manner:

1. Use simple sentences: Use short and simple sentences to convey information. Avoid using complex or abstract language that may be difficult for individuals with autism to understand.

2. Focus on concrete information: Provide concrete information about the target behavior or situation. Use specific examples and avoid vague or ambiguous language.

3. Use visual supports: Visual supports, such as pictures or symbols, can enhance understanding for individuals with autism. Include visuals that represent the information being conveyed in the social story.

4. Break down complex concepts: If the target behavior or situation involves complex concepts, break them down into smaller, more manageable parts. Present each part separately and provide clear explanations.

Using Visuals to Enhance Social Stories

Visuals can enhance social stories by providing a visual representation of the information being conveyed. They can help individuals with autism make connections between the story and real-life situations, and enhance their understanding of social expectations and behaviors.

There are different types of visuals that can be used in social stories, including:

1. Photographs: Photographs can be used to depict real-life situations and people. They provide a realistic representation of the target behavior or situation.

2. Drawings or illustrations: Drawings or illustrations can be used to depict abstract concepts or situations that may be difficult to photograph. They can be created by hand or using digital tools.

3. Symbols or icons: Symbols or icons can be used to represent specific actions or concepts. They provide a visual representation of the information being conveyed and can help individuals with autism make connections between the story and real-life situations.

4. Visual schedules: Visual schedules can be used to provide a visual representation of the steps involved in a specific behavior or situation. They can help individuals with autism understand the sequence of events and what is expected of them.

Incorporating Personalization in Social Stories

Personalization is important in social stories to make them more relatable and meaningful for individuals with autism. Personalized social stories are more likely to capture the individual's attention and engage them in the learning process.

Here are some tips for incorporating personalization into social stories:

1. Use the individual's name: Use the individual's name throughout the social story to make it more personal. This helps the individual feel connected to the story and increases their engagement.

2. Include specific details: Include specific details that are relevant to the individual's experiences. For example, if you are creating a social story about going to the dentist, include details about the individual's dentist and what they can expect during their visit.

3. Use familiar settings or characters: Use familiar settings or characters in the social story to make it more relatable. For example, if you are creating a social story about going to school, use pictures of the individual's school or classmates.

4. Incorporate the individual's interests: Incorporate the individual's interests into the social story to increase their engagement. For example, if the individual is interested in dinosaurs, include pictures of dinosaurs in the social story.

Addressing Challenging Behaviors in Social Stories

Social stories can be used to address challenging behaviors by providing clear and concrete information about appropriate behavior and strategies for success. Here are some examples of how to address specific behaviors in social stories:

1. Hitting or biting: If the individual engages in hitting or biting, create a social story that explains why this behavior is not acceptable and provides alternative strategies for expressing frustration or anger.

2. Meltdowns or tantrums: If the individual has meltdowns or tantrums, create a social story that explains what triggers these behaviors and provides strategies for self-regulation and calming down.

3. Obsessive or repetitive behaviors: If the individual engages in obsessive or repetitive behaviors, create a social story that explains why these behaviors may be disruptive or harmful and provides alternative activities or coping strategies.

4. Difficulty with transitions: If the individual has difficulty with transitions, create a social story that explains what to expect during transitions and provides strategies for managing anxiety or stress.

How to Use Social Stories in Different Settings (Home, School, Community)

Social stories can be used in different settings to help individuals with autism navigate various social situations. Here are some examples of how to use social stories in different settings:

1. Home: Use social stories at home to teach and reinforce appropriate behaviors and routines. For example, create a social story about bedtime routines or mealtime expectations.

2. School: Use social stories at school to prepare individuals with autism for new experiences or events. For example, create a social story about starting a new school year or going on a field trip.

3. Community: Use social stories in the community to help individuals with autism understand and navigate different social situations. For example, create a social story about going to the grocery store or visiting a park.

Adapt the social stories to fit the specific needs and experiences of the individual with autism in each setting.

Evaluating the Effectiveness of Social Stories

It is important to evaluate the effectiveness of social stories to ensure that they are meeting the needs of the individual with autism. Here are some tips for evaluating the effectiveness of social stories:

1. Observe behavior: Observe the individual's behavior in the target situation before and after using the social story. Look for changes in behavior or improvements in social skills.

2. Collect data: Collect data on the individual's behavior using objective measures, such as frequency or duration of specific behaviors. Compare the data before and after using the social story to determine if there have been any improvements.

3. Seek feedback: Seek feedback from the individual with autism, as well as from parents, teachers, or other professionals who work with the individual. Ask for their observations and opinions on the effectiveness of the social story.

4. Make adjustments as needed: If the social story is not having the desired effect, make adjustments to the content or format. Consider seeking input from professionals who specialize in working with individuals with autism.

Collaborating with Professionals for Successful Social Story Implementation

Collaboration with professionals is important for successful implementation of social stories. Professionals who specialize in working with individuals with autism can provide valuable insights and guidance throughout the process.

Here are some tips for collaborating with professionals:

1. Seek input and feedback: Seek input and feedback from professionals when creating social stories. They can provide guidance on content, format, and strategies for implementation.

2. Share progress and challenges: Share progress and challenges with professionals to get their input and support. They can help troubleshoot any issues that arise and provide additional strategies or resources.

3. Attend training or workshops: Attend training or workshops offered by professionals to learn more about social stories and how to effectively implement them. This can help build your knowledge and skills in using social stories with individuals with autism.

4. Establish open communication: Establish open communication with professionals to ensure that everyone is on the same page and working towards the same goals. Regularly communicate updates, ask questions, and seek guidance as needed.

Social stories are a valuable tool for individuals with autism, providing a structured and visual way to teach social skills and promote understanding of social expectations. By addressing the specific needs of individuals with autism, social stories help them navigate social situations and develop appropriate behaviors. By following the step-by-step guide and incorporating the tips provided in this blog post, you can create effective social stories that enhance the social skills and overall well-being of individuals with autism. Remember to evaluate the effectiveness of the social stories and collaborate with professionals for successful implementation.

Chapter 30: From Awkward to Awesome: How Social Thinking Can Transform Your Life

Social thinking is a crucial aspect of human interaction and communication. It refers to the ability to understand and interpret the thoughts, feelings, and intentions of others, as well as to consider how our own actions and words may impact those around us. Social thinking plays a vital role in personal relationships, as well as in various aspects of life, including career success and emotional intelligence. By developing and honing our social thinking skills, we can improve our relationships, navigate social situations more effectively, and enhance our overall well-being.

What is social thinking and why is it important?

Social thinking can be defined as the cognitive process through which individuals interpret and understand social cues, make sense of others' behaviors and intentions, and adjust their own behavior accordingly. It involves being aware of one's own thoughts and emotions, as well as being able to take the perspective of others. Social thinking is important because it allows us to navigate social situations effectively, build and maintain meaningful relationships, and understand the impact of our actions on others.

The impact of social thinking on personal relationships

Social thinking has a significant impact on personal relationships. It affects how we communicate, understand others' perspectives, and respond to their needs. When we are able to engage in social thinking, we are more likely to have successful and fulfilling relationships. For example, by considering the thoughts and feelings of our partner during a disagreement, we can approach the situation with empathy and understanding rather than defensiveness or aggression. Social thinking also helps us recognize when someone may be feeling sad or upset, allowing us to offer support and comfort.

Overcoming social anxiety through social thinking

Social anxiety is a common issue that many people face when it comes to social interactions. However, social thinking can be a powerful tool in overcoming this anxiety. By practicing social thinking skills, individuals can learn to challenge negative thoughts and beliefs that contribute to their anxiety. For example, instead of assuming that others are judging them or thinking negatively about them, individuals can use social thinking to consider alternative explanations for others' behaviors. This can help reduce anxiety and increase confidence in social situations.

Developing empathy and emotional intelligence through social thinking

Empathy and emotional intelligence are essential skills for building and maintaining healthy relationships. Social thinking plays a crucial role in developing these skills. By being aware of our own thoughts and emotions, we can better understand and empathize with the experiences of others. Social thinking also helps us recognize and interpret nonverbal cues, such as facial expressions and body language, which are important indicators of others' emotions. By incorporating social thinking into our interactions, we can improve our ability to connect with others on an emotional level.

The role of self-awareness in social thinking

Self-awareness is a fundamental aspect of social thinking. It involves being conscious of our own thoughts, feelings, and behaviors, as well as how they may impact others. By developing self-awareness, we can better understand our own strengths and weaknesses in social situations. This allows us to make adjustments and improvements as needed. For example, if we notice that we tend to dominate conversations or interrupt others frequently, we can use self-awareness to recognize this behavior and work on listening more actively.

How social thinking can improve communication skills

Communication is a key component of social interactions, and social thinking plays a crucial role in improving communication skills. By being aware of others' perspectives and considering their needs, we can communicate more effectively and avoid misunderstandings. Social thinking also helps us recognize when it is appropriate to ask questions or seek clarification, rather than making assumptions. By incorporating social thinking into our communication, we can build stronger connections with others and foster more meaningful conversations.

Building confidence and self-esteem with social thinking

Social thinking can have a positive impact on confidence and self-esteem. By being aware of our own thoughts and emotions, we can challenge negative self-talk and beliefs that may be holding us back. Social thinking also helps us recognize our strengths and accomplishments, which can boost confidence. By using social thinking to approach social situations with empathy and understanding, we can build positive relationships and receive validation and support from others, further enhancing our self-esteem.

The connection between social thinking and career success

Social thinking is not only important in personal relationships but also in the workplace. It plays a crucial role in building professional relationships, collaborating with colleagues, and effectively communicating ideas. By using social thinking skills, individuals can navigate office politics, understand the needs and motivations of their coworkers, and build strong networks. Social thinking also helps individuals adapt to different work environments and cultures, which is essential for career success.

Using social thinking to navigate social situations and avoid misunderstandings

Social thinking is a valuable tool for navigating social situations and avoiding misunderstandings. By being aware of others' perspectives and considering their needs, we can adjust our behavior and communication style accordingly. For example, if we notice that someone seems uncomfortable or disengaged in a conversation, we can use social thinking to adapt our approach and make them feel more at ease. By incorporating social thinking into our interactions, we can reduce the likelihood of misunderstandings and foster more positive connections with others.

The benefits of incorporating social thinking into daily life

Incorporating social thinking into daily life has numerous benefits. It allows us to build stronger relationships, communicate more effectively, and navigate social situations with confidence. Social thinking also enhances our emotional intelligence and empathy, which are essential skills for personal growth and well-being. By using social thinking in various aspects of life, such as at work or in personal relationships, we can experience greater satisfaction and fulfillment.

Tips and strategies for improving social thinking skills

Improving social thinking skills takes practice and effort. Here are some tips and strategies to help enhance social thinking:

1. Practice active listening: Pay attention to what others are saying and make an effort to understand their perspective.

2. Observe nonverbal cues: Pay attention to facial expressions, body language, and tone of voice to better understand others' emotions and intentions.

3. Reflect on your own thoughts and emotions: Take time to reflect on your own thoughts and emotions before responding in social situations.

4. Seek feedback: Ask trusted friends or family members for feedback on your social interactions to gain insight into areas for improvement.

5. Read books or take courses on social thinking: There are many resources available that can provide guidance and strategies for improving social thinking skills.

Social thinking is a crucial aspect of human interaction and communication. By developing and honing our social thinking skills, we can improve our relationships, navigate social situations more effectively, and enhance our overall well-being. Social thinking allows us to understand and interpret the thoughts, feelings, and intentions of others, as well as to consider how our own actions and words may impact those around us. By incorporating social thinking into our daily lives, we can experience the benefits of stronger relationships, improved communication skills, and increased empathy and emotional intelligence.

Don't miss out!

Visit the website below and you can sign up to receive emails whenever Travis Breeding publishes a new book. There's no charge and no obligation.

https://books2read.com/r/B-A-CBXDB-FYGXC

BOOKS 2 READ

Connecting independent readers to independent writers.

Did you love *Twice Exceptional: Navigating Life with Autism and Gomez Lopez Hernandez Syndrome*? Then you should read *Dancing With Shadows: How To Turn Your Fears Into Powerful Allies*[1] by Travis Breeding!

[2]

Step into the captivating world of Travis Breeding as he fearlessly unveils the intricate layers of his life in 'Echoes of the Mind: A Schizophrenic's Odyssey.' In this compelling autobiography, Breeding takes readers on an extraordinary journey through the labyrinth of his mind, navigating the tumultuous terrain of schizophrenia with raw honesty and unwavering courage.

From the early whispers of auditory hallucinations to the bewildering onset of delusions, Breeding candidly shares the harrowing experiences that shaped his reality. Through the lens of his own

---

1. https://books2read.com/u/bo9MkV

2. https://books2read.com/u/bo9MkV

narrative, readers gain profound insight into the inner workings of schizophrenia, demystifying misconceptions and shedding light on the profound complexities of the human psyche.

As Breeding delves into the depths of his psyche, he unearths the poignant moments of triumph amidst adversity. Through relentless determination and unwavering resilience, he transcends the confines of his diagnosis, forging a path towards healing and self-discovery. Along the way, he grapples with the pervasive stigma surrounding mental illness, challenging societal perceptions and advocating for greater understanding and acceptance.

'Echoes of the Mind' is more than just a memoir—it is a testament to the indomitable spirit of the human experience. With poignant prose and searing authenticity, Breeding invites readers to embark on a transformative odyssey of self-reflection and empathy. This powerful memoir serves as a beacon of hope for individuals navigating the complexities of mental illness and a poignant reminder of the enduring power of the human spirit.

Read more at breedingautismconsulting.com.

Also by Travis Breeding

Harmony in Flux: Navigating Bi-Polar Brilliance
The Friendship Rainbow
The Great Kindergarten Adventure: A Story about Going to School
with Autism
The Magic Forest Adventure
Unlocking Brilliance: Navigating Autism and Applied Behavior
Analysis Towards a Radiant Future
Decoding Love: Navigating Dating and Relationships on the Autism
Spectrum
Echoes of a Late Diagnosis: Unveiling the Spectrum Within
From Theory to Practice: Implementing Effective Autism
Interventions St
The Amazing Adventures of Aiden and His Asperger's Superpowers
The Magical Adventures of Lily and the Enchanted Forest
Unlocking Potential: A Journey Of Discovery Through ABA Therapy
Unlocking Potential: Navigating Employment for Neurodiverse
Talent
Unlocking the Spectrum: A Journey through Applied Behavior
Analysis from an Autistic Perspective
Unlocking The Spectrum: Navigating The Complexity Of Autism
With Advanced Strategies And Insights
Beyond The Spectrum: Insights From Autistic Adults
Beyond The Stereotypes
Breaking Barriers: Navigating Autism With Therapeutic Insight
Celebrating Neurodiversity

Watch for more at breedingautismconsulting.com.

About the Author

Travis is the author of over 50 books about autism spectrum disorder. He travelst he country sharing the mission of making the world a better place for autistic individuals. In his spare time Travis enjoys writing, walking, and watching sports.

Read more at breedingautismconsulting.com.